FOCUS ON
FLUENCY

A Meaning-Based Approach

Nancy Lee Cecil

CALIFORNIA STATE UNIVERSITY, SACRAMENTO

Holcomb Hathaway, Publishers
Scottsdale, Arizona

FLUENCY AND TECHNOLOGY   103

FLUENCY AND ASSESSMENT   117

Across the United States, fluency has become an important topic. In 2000, the National Reading Panel presented fluency as one of the five building blocks to successful reading. Soon after that, educators in every state began to grapple with the issue of how to create more fluent readers and writers. Journal articles discussed how to increase fluency and professional literacy conferences soon devoted major strands to instruction in fluency. Despite this increased attention on fluency, however, discussions continue about what exactly is meant by the concept *fluency.*

Fluency in literacy is commonly defined as *the ability to read and write accurately and rapidly and, in the case of reading, with appropriate expression.* Too often, however, fluency instruction is operationalized in classrooms through having children endlessly practice reading passages as fast as they can or having them reread material they have just read without giving them any real reason to do so. *Focus on Fluency: A Meaning-Based Approach* is designed to ensure that meaning and fluency remain fully intertwined. We must teach children, especially when they are learning to read fluently, that the essential purpose of reading is always to gain meaning from the printed page.

This book is a supplementary text for preservice and inservice teachers searching for best practices with which to promote fluency in their K–6 learners. It will help educators develop effective ways to promote fluent reading and writing, thereby engaging children in meaningful experiences with text and motivating them to read. Such experiences create a wonderful cycle of practice leading to more fluent reading, and more fluent reading leading to a desire to read more—and thus more practice!

The contents and organization of this book reflect the belief that teachers will not *own* a method or procedure—that is, will not fully incorporate a practical activity into their repertoire of teaching methods—unless they understand the reason behind the technique and see how it fits into the larger goal of creating literate human beings. In addition, preservice and practicing teachers studying the art and science of teaching need real examples of classroom practice that make sense to them. In this book, educators will find explanations and clear purposes for each instructional activity and step-by-step examples of how the activity might be used in the classroom setting.

Children can experience difficulty with fluency at any point in their literacy development. Children for whom English is a second language may experience difficulties, but so may those who are native speakers. To assist teachers working with culturally diverse children at a variety of skill levels, I have included instructional activities easily modified for grade levels from primary through middle school as well as activities appropriate to English learners.

SPECIAL FEATURES

To go beyond techniques to foster rereading, the most commonly accepted way to increase fluency, this book includes the following chapters and special features:

- **Chapters on choral reading and drama.** Providing authentic purposes for reading motivates children to read, which is the best way to give them the practice they need to become more fluent readers. These two chapters offer specific activities to bring the excitement of drama and choral reading into the classroom.

- **Chapter on writing.** Reading and writing are reciprocal processes in literacy, and improvement in one will lead to improvement in the other. This chapter focuses on increasing fluency in writing, a vital dimension of literacy.

- **Chapter on fluency and technology.** In this chapter I explore ways to use exemplary computer programs to provide additional fluency practice. The chapter addresses how to select such programs and how to integrate them into an existing literacy program.

- **Additional resources.** Appendices include lists of children's literature suitable for children to read aloud, commercial plays and readers theatre materials, songs and song books, books and anthologies for poetry reading, and web addresses for software discussed in the text.

ACKNOWLEDGMENTS

This book has come to fruition thanks to my colleagues, my students, and the teachers with whom I work. On-going discussions of theory and practice with these outstanding professionals allowed me to explore, question, and modify my views on teaching fluency. They helped me in developing techniques that are efficient and enjoyable to children and keep the goal of gaining meaning from the printed page always at the forefront of any instructional activity.

I want to extend my sincere appreciation to the following individuals, who reviewed this book in earlier versions and offered constructive suggestions for improving it. My thanks to Gwynne Ash, University of Delaware; Sara Ann Beach, The University of Oklahoma; Leah Kinniburgh, Lynn University; Dorothy Leal, Ohio University; Jennifer McGregor, Tarleton State University; Virginia Modla, LaSalle University; Beth Anne Pruitt, Eastern Kentucky University; Mary Strong, Widener University; and Catana Turner, University of Virginia–Wise.

Thank you to my husband, Gary, for his support of my writing and unwavering belief in my ability to juggle writing, teaching, and our home life. You have always been my greatest fan!

A special thank you to everyone at Holcomb Hathaway for their dedication to this project. Colette Kelly, my editor, has long shared my vision for what literacy can and should be. Thanks also to Sally Scott for her good eye and detailed oversight of the project.

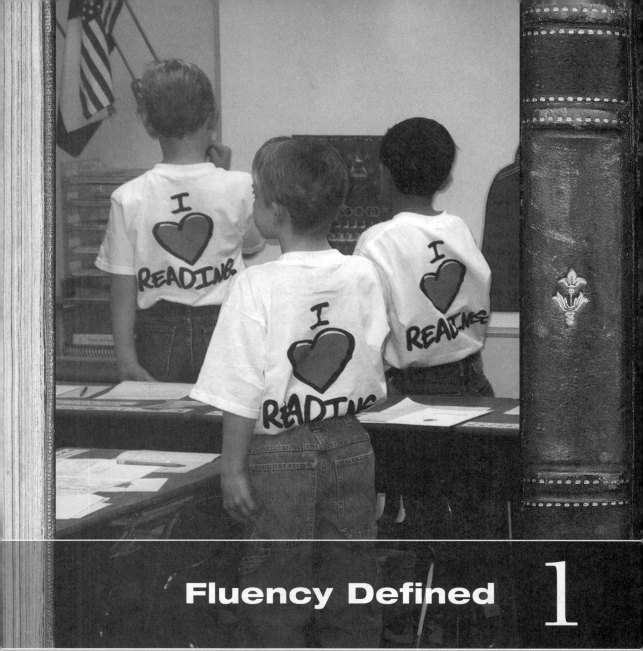

Fluency Defined 1

In the beginning stages of learning to read, a child must depend heavily on decoding abilities to be able to pronounce words. These decoding abilities include breaking words apart into pronounceable components and putting the appropriate sound with its corresponding symbol(s). In a nutshell, as the child gains repeated practice in performing these requisite reading tasks, she learns to recognize more and more words automatically, accurately, and rapidly, and thus becomes what we can call a "fluent reader" (Kuhn & Stahl, 2000). Similarly, when the child is able to spell words accurately and rapidly and to use words to compose her ideas, we can say she has become a "fluent writer."

WHY IS FLUENCY IMPORTANT?

Fluency, in part, is about developing a large sight vocabulary of words that have been met and decoded, or simply memorized, during one's academic lifetime. Proficient adult readers, for example, are able to read about 50,000 words fairly rapidly—words that we have seen often enough, through exposure to roughly 4 million words read every year, that they are part of our sight vocabulary. On the other hand, struggling readers who are not fluent have very few words in their sight vocabulary, and thus they must spend an exorbitant amount of time and energy sounding out most of the words they read, time and energy that could be more joyfully spent thinking about the personal meaning of the text (Armbruster, Lehr, & Osborn, 2001). Indeed, without fluency and accuracy at the level of the word, there will always be constraints on comprehension (Adams, 1990; Adams & Bruck, 1995).

The National Reading Panel (2000) has underscored the importance of fluency by naming it one of the important components of early reading, along with comprehension, phonemic awareness, phonics, and vocabulary. The research behind the need for fluent reading is abundant and the results clear. According to the most commonly held theory, the degree or amount of attention readers can devote to cognitive tasks such as reading is limited. Reading requires children to accomplish at least two critical tasks: they must be able to use strategies to figure out the words, and they must be able to comprehend the text. Given the limited attentional resources available to any reader, according to this theory, attention used to decode text is no longer available for comprehending. Therefore, readers who spend inordinate amounts of time working to decode words—even successfully—may lack the focus necessary to use comprehension strategies (LaBerge & Samuels, 1974).

The major goal of all literacy instruction, obviously, is to create proficient readers and writers. Proficient readers, by definition, read quickly and effortlessly, and they decode most words automatically. When they read aloud or silently to themselves, they also read with expression, appropriate phrasing, and intonation, inserting pauses as one typically does in conversation, while emphasizing important words.

Similarly, proficient writers are those who write effortlessly and accurately. Besides being able to generate ideas quickly, they demonstrate automaticity with the conventions of print, particularly the ability to spell accurately and rapidly.

Fluency instruction, therefore, will ideally focus on helping children to read words and phrases quickly and automatically, with appropriate expression. Connecting reading and writing when planning fluency instruction has practical benefits as well. The two processes are believed to be mutually beneficial, as writing contributes to a child's reading fluency development, and reading contributes to a child's writing fluency development (Shanahan, 1988). The hope in this developmental process is that once the child has attained fluency, that child can then turn her cognitive energy to the more critical issues of gaining meaning from the printed page—reading to learn and for enjoyment.

DEFINING FLUENCY

What exactly makes up the ability to read a passage fluently? Although teachers and researchers have yet to agree on minor elements of reading fluency, most can agree on its essential components. Most researchers would agree that there is much more to fluency than simply being able to read a series of words correctly. Rasinski (2003) defines fluency as "the ability to read accurately, quickly, effortlessly, and with appropriate expression and meaning" (p. 19). Reading researchers currently studying fluency also consider the following often overlooked features: (1) accuracy of decoding; (2) appropriate use of pitch, juncture, and stress in one's voice; and (3) appropriate text phrasing, or "chunking" (Allington, 2001; LaBerge & Samuels, 1974; National Reading Panel, 2000; Perfetti, 1985; Stanovich, 1980, 1986). Thus, a fluent reader should be someone who can decode the words in the text accurately and with relative ease, but who also reads with correct phrasing, appropriate intonation, and at a reasonably rapid rate so as to facilitate comprehension of a text. As children become fluent readers, they build a stockpile of words they do not recognize but can easily figure out and a larger store of other words that they begin to recognize instantly. If readers come to unfamiliar words, they learn to use decoding techniques to hypothesize the pronunciation of the word either orally or silently.

For the purposes of this book, we will define fluency operationally by using the three critical components of fluency identified by Hudson, Lane, and Pullen (2005): rate, accuracy, and "prosody," a broad term that encompasses all the rhythmic, expressive, and conversational characteristics of speech summarized in Exhibit 1.1.

exhibit 1.1 Attributes of fluent readers: A summary.

Fluent readers read:

- Effortlessly
- Smoothly
- Accurately
- Quickly
- With automatic decoding (automaticity)
- Flexibly, for different purposes
- With appropriate expression

- With tone and intonation
- With appropriate phrasing, or "chunking"
- With meaning
- With appropriate pauses and emphasis
- Without undue laboring over decoding
- Following punctuation in text

Rate

Rapid and effortless decoding strategies are important because, when a child reads words with automaticity, her remaining cognitive energy can be used for comprehension, as has been stated previously. Additionally, much correlational evidence suggests that increased reading rate is related to higher levels of comprehension, at least in average and struggling readers (Chard, Vaughn, & Tyler, 2002; Tenenbaum & Wolking, 1989). But researchers have identified other reasons why reading rapidly is important. Being slow to identify and process visual information puts children at a distinct disadvantage, according to Lovett, Steinbach, and Frijters (2000). They propose that in one second of reading, a fluent reader is able to identify and process about five words of text—which translates to about 300 words per minute—whereas a less rapid reader may identify and process only 230 words per minute, approximately a quarter fewer than the fluent reader. Moreover, children who process all visual material more quickly tend to get more out of the time spent reading and thus have an easier time developing other skills needed to make them proficient readers. It therefore seems that while reading speed is not the most critical issue in becoming a proficient reader, it *does* matter (Rasinski, 2000).

Accuracy

For accurate reading to occur, a child must have a large store of words that he recognizes by sight. He must also possess the ability to figure out unfamiliar words by means of a sequentially executed process whereby he breaks words into their component parts and then puts corresponding sounds to the letters in each word part. The inaccurate reading of words resulting from limited sight word knowledge or insufficient decoding strategies has obvious negative consequences on reading comprehension and fluency. When many words are read incorrectly, it seems axiomatic that the reader would be apt to misinterpret text and misunderstand the author's intent. In the 2002 Oral Fluency Study, researchers found, not unexpectedly, that when children made errors that affected the meaning of the text, comprehension was affected more than when the errors did not affect the meaning of the text; however, they also noted that children rarely make reading errors that do *not* affect the meaning of text (National Assessment Governing Board, 2002). Therefore, a reader who is able to decode most of the text accurately will be more likely to get meaning from the printed page and, thus, enjoy the activity.

Prosody

Prosody, as defined by many reading experts, is the reader's ability to recognize phrases rather than to read word by word. Expression, a subset of prosody, is the reader's ability to make the written word sound like "real speech" by using the correct intonation of voice (such as raising the voice on questions, etc.). When a fluent reader who is reading aloud has "correct" prosody, it sounds much like conversational speaking. Richards (2000) refers to this aspect of fluency as "the ability to read in expressive rhythmic and melodic patterns" (p. 535). In contrast, children who are not fluent readers are often described as reading without any expression, or with pauses that do not correspond to the natural pauses one takes in normal discourse. It is not clear whether correct prosody is a "cause" or an "effect" of comprehension, or whether the relationship is synergistic. When one listens to a reader with correct prosody, it certainly appears that understanding has occurred, whereas someone who listens to a reader who pauses inappropriately and speaks monotonously will be hard-pressed to believe that the reader understands the material. Kuhn and Stahl (2003) support this observation by theorizing that prosodic reading is "evidence" that a certain level of comprehension has taken place.

A BRIEF HISTORY OF FLUENCY INSTRUCTION

Reading fluency—the ability to read smoothly, at a reasonable rate, and with expression—has historically been acknowledged as an important goal in becoming a proficient and strategic reader (Allington, 1983, 2001; Dowhower, 1991; Hudson, Lane, & Pullen, 2005;

Klenk & Kibby, 2000; National Reading Panel., 2000; Opitz & Rasinski, 1998; Rasinski, 2000, 2003; Rasinski & Padak, 1996; Reutzel & Cooter, 2000; Reutzel, Hollingsworth, & Eldredge, 1994). However, in the early 1900s there was a shift in emphasis away from proficient oral reading and toward silent reading for personal purposes, so the goal of developing fluent *oral* readers all but disappeared from the reading curriculum. In fact, this was so much the case that it prompted Allington (1983) to declare oral reading fluency to be an often-neglected goal of reading instruction. Researchers found that many reading methods textbooks and basal reader teacher's manuals in elementary classrooms were providing little or no guidance for developing oral fluency as an important part of comprehensive reading instruction programs. Likewise, visitors to many elementary school classrooms in much of the latter twentieth century would often observe little attention to oral reading and fluency instruction in daily lessons.

CURRENT PRACTICES FOR TEACHING AND ASSESSING FLUENCY

In the past few years, elementary schools in California and other states have begun to spend a considerable amount of time on the instruction and assessment of fluency, based on research that suggests that, once a reader becomes so fluent that all decoding is automatic, she can then turn her attention to the more critical issues of comprehension and true enjoyment and engagement with text (Carnine, Carnine, & Gersten, 1984; Chall, 1967; Griffith & Rasinski, 2004; Lesgold & Curtis, 1981; Reutzel & Hollingsworth, 1991). Indeed, one of the primary goals of reading instruction has now become to foster fluency (Wren, 2005).

How this important literacy skill is sometimes operationalized in schools is causing many educators considerable concern. While the majority of instruction has been carefully considered to keep the joy and meaning in literacy, the following unfortunate scenario, observed in a third-grade classroom in California, reflects what has also become an all-too-common practice:

The teacher gives a student a short passage to read. (S)he tells the child, "Read this passage as quickly as you can. Now begin!" The teacher then clicks a stopwatch, times the reading, and records the number of words the child reads correctly in one minute, stopping the child when that minute has expired. The stopwatch is stopped, the child returns to her seat, and the procedure is repeated with another child until all children have been assessed in fluency in this manner. Although comprehension strategies may be taught at other times of the day, they are rarely assessed or in any way considered during this brief activity.

To the many children who have been given an expedient fluency assessment in this manner, multiple times during the school year, only one erroneous conclusion can be drawn concerning their experience: "*Good* reading means *fast* reading."

To add to this situation, subsequent instructional activities designed to develop the skills of fluency often consist of assigning students to read the same story several times, without offering any *authentic* purpose for the ensuing readings. This misinterpretation of the repeated-readings approach to increasing fluency, which is effective in more creative contexts, does little to promote reading enjoyment. At best, such practices turn children off to reading as a pleasurable pursuit; at worst, children are made to feel that such repetitive, meaningless tasks are little more than mild punishment. And when children are turned off to reading, they read less, and thus the practice needed to become a fluent reader never occurs.

Furthermore, benchmarks for fluency have been established in many districts, such as the San Juan District in California, in which a student's reading report card grade will often depend solely on the number of words per minute the child is able to read accurately, with no mention of the child's ability to recall what was read.

WHAT CAN BE DONE TO IMPROVE FLUENCY?

I believe that the optimal way to increase fluency is to help children learn to love reading so that they will choose to read often in their spare time, in and away from school. Reading practice—like practice in anything, whether it is typing, skiing, or speaking a second language— will increase ability in that endeavor. Children will learn to love to read, and thus read and practice *more*, if they feel they are successful in doing so, and if they are provided with an abundance of books on their interest and ability level. Such recreational reading will provide the critical reading practice that is necessary to create readers who read rapidly and accurately, with appropriate prosody. However, many children will also need some specific, direct instruction on one or more of these three areas in order to become more fluent, even though they are doing a great deal of recreational reading.

With this in mind, some activities in the remainder of this book offer a host of specific instructional recommendations. Certain suggestions and activities provide authentic reasons for reading and rereading orally as well as silently. Such activities have been carefully chosen not only for their effective fostering of fluency, but also because they represent what we know to be the most effective literacy practices to date, such as:

- making predictions
- providing for diverse learning styles
- eliciting personal responses to literature
- making connections to one's own life and culture

An entire chapter (Chapter 8) addresses how technology can be used to foster fluency proficiency. Instructional activities and discussions in other chapters speak to underlying elements that cause problems in decoding words, resulting in increased difficulty with fluency. I devote Chapter 7 to fluency in writing, as the two cognitive processes are reciprocal; in other words, practice in writing ultimately leads to increased fluency in reading, and vice versa. The assessment chapter, Chapter 9, offers a model designed to help teachers, and the children themselves, discover what skills must be developed in order to allow children to read rapidly, accurately, and effortlessly. Also provided in Chapter 9 are an informal assessment of word writing proficiency—the Word Writing CAFÉ—and a checklist for early writing fluency. *All* the activities in this book have been expressly designed to provide enjoyable experiences with literacy, in order to create children who can read and write fluently and choose to do so—far beyond the classroom doors.

REFERENCES

Adams, M. J. (1990). *Beginning to read: Thinking and learning about print.* Cambridge, MA: MIT Press.

Adams, M. J., & Bruck, M. (1995). Resolving the "great debate." *American Educator, 19,* 10–20.

Allington, R. (2001). What really matters for struggling readers: Designing research-based programs. Boston: Longman.

Armbruster, B. B., Lehr, E., & Osborn, J. (2001). *Put reading first: The research building blocks for teaching children to read. Kindergarten through grade 3.* Washington, DC: National Institute for Literacy.

Block, C. C. (2000). *Teaching the language arts: Expanding thinking through student-centered instruction,* 3rd ed. Boston: Allyn & Bacon.

Carnine, L., Carnine, D., & Gersten, R. (1984). Analysis of oral reading errors made by economically disadvantaged students taught with a synthetic phonics approach. *Reading Research Quarterly, 19,* 343–356.

Chall, J. S. (1967). *Learning to read: The great debate.* New York: McGraw-Hill.

Chard, D. J., Vaughn, S., & Tyler, B. J. (2002). A synthesis of research on effective interventions for building reading fluency with elementary students with learning disabilities. *Journal of Learning Disabilities, 35,* 386–486.

Crawley, S. J., & Merritt, K. (2000). *Remediating reading difficulties,* 3rd ed. Boston: McGraw-Hill.

Dowhower, S. L. (1991). Speaking of prosody: Fluency's unattended bedfellow. *Theory into Practice, 30,* 165–175.

Griffith, L. W., & Rasinski, T. V. (2004). A focus on fluency: How one teacher incorporated fluency with her reading curriculum. *The Reading Teacher, 58*(2), 126–137.

Hudson, R. F., Lane, H. B., & Pullen, P. C. (2005). Reading fluency and assessment: What, why and how? *The Reading Teacher, 58*(8), 702–714.

Klenk, L., & Kibby, M. W. (2000). Re-mediating reading difficulties: Appraising the past, reconciling the present, constructing the future. In M. L. Kamil, P. B. Mosenthal, P. D. Pearson, & R. Barr (Eds.), *Handbook of Reading Research,* vol. 3. Mahwah, NJ: Lawrence Erlbaum.

Kuhn, M. R., & Stahl, S. A. (2000). Fluency: A review of developmental and remedial practices. *Journal of Educational Psychology, 95,* 3–21.

LaBerge, D., & Samuels, S. J. (1974). Toward a theory of automatic information processing in reading. *Cognitive Psychology, 6,* 293–323.

Lesgold, A. M., & Curtis, M. E. (1981). Learning to read words efficiently. In A. M. Lesgold & C. A. Perfetti (Eds.), *Interactive processes in reading.* Hillsdale, NJ: Lawrence Erlbaum.

Lovett, M. W., Steinbach, K. A., & Frijters, J. C. (2000). Remediating the core deficits of developmental reading disability: A double deficit perspective. *Journal of Learning Disabilities, 33*(4), 334–358.

National Assessment Governing Board. (2002). Reading framework for the 2003 National Assessment of Educational Progress. Available at: www.nagb.org/pubs/reading_framework/tok.html.

National Reading Panel. (2000). Report of the National Reading Panel: Teaching children to read: An evidence-based assessment of the scientific research literature on reading and its implications for reading instruction. Washington, DC: National Institute of Child Health and Human Development, National Institutes of Health.

Opitz, M. F., & Rasinski, T. V. (1998). *Good-bye round robin: 25 effective oral reading strategies.* Portsmouth, NH: Heinemann.

Perfetti, C. (1985). *Reading ability.* New York: Oxford University Press.

Rasinski, T. (1989). Fluency for everyone: Incorporating fluency instruction in the classroom. *The Reading Teacher, 42*(9), 690–693.

Rasinski, T. (1990a). Effects of repeated reading and listening-while-reading on reading fluency. *The Journal of Educational Research, 83*(3), 147–150.

Rasinski, T. (1990b). Investigating measure of reading fluency. *Educational Research Quarterly, 14*(3), 37–44.

Rasinski, T. V. (2000). Speed does matter. *The Reading Teacher, 54*(2), 146–151.

Rasinski, T. (2003). *The fluent reader*. New York: Scholastic.

Rasinski, T. V., & Padak, N. (1996). Five lessons to increase reading fluency. In L. R. Putnam (Ed.), *How to become a better reading teacher: Strategies for assessment and intervention*. Columbus, OH: Merrill/Prentice Hall.

Rasinski, T. V., Padak, N. M., Linek, W., & Sturtevant, E. (1994). Effects of fluency development on urban second-grade readers. *The Journal of Educational Research, 87*(3), 158–165.

Reutzel, D. R., & Cooter, R. B. (2003). *Strategies for reading assessment and instruction*, 2nd ed. Upper Saddle River, NJ: Merrill.

Reutzel, D. R., & Hollingsworth, P. M. (1991). Reading comprehension skills: Testing the skills distinctiveness hypothesis. *Reading Research and Instructions, 30*, 32–46.

Reutzel, D. R., Hollingsworth, P. M., & Eldredge, J. L. (1994). Oral reading instruction: The impact on student reading development. *Reading Research Quarterly, 23*, 40–62.

Richards, M. (2000). Be a good detective: Solve the case of oral fluency. *The Reading Teacher, 53*, 534–539.

Shanahan, T. (1988). The reading-writing relationship: Seven instructional principles. *The Reading Teacher, 41*, 636–647.

Stanovich, K. E. (1980). Toward an interactive-compensatory model of individual differences in the development of reading fluency. *Reading Research Quarterly, 16*, 32–71.

Stanovich, K. E. (1986). Matthew effects in reading: Some consequences of individual differences in the acquisition of reading. *Reading Research Quarterly, 22*, 360–407.

Tenenbaum, H. A., & Wolking, W. D. (1989). Effects of oral reading rate on intraverbal responding. *The Analysis of Verbal Behavior, 7*, 83–89.

Wren, S. (2005). Developing research-based resources for the balanced reading teacher: Fluency. From BalancedReading.com. Available at: www.balanced reading.com/fluency.html.

Oral Reading and Fluency $\quad$ 2

W ith fluency so critical to reading success, as evidence suggests, what can be done to help children become fluent readers and writers? The most basic answer is to give them practice, practice, and more practice with every facet of literacy. But a further question remains: Will just any kind of practice do? If not, what kind of practice will be the most effective? To answer this question, it is helpful to examine the report of the National Reading Panel (2000). The Panel analyzed an abundance of research concerning two instructional approaches widely used in classrooms to foster reading fluency: "repeated oral reading" and "sustained silent reading." As a result of this analysis, the Panel concluded that much evidence supports the practice of repeated reading in elementary classrooms. This practice offers children opportunities for the reading practice necessary to become fluent readers. Repeated oral reading requires a child to read a passage out loud several times, with guidance and feedback, to a listener who is a fluent reader. This approach, and other related instructional activities for developing oral reading fluency, will be explored in the remainder of this chapter. Independent silent reading, the approach recognized by the National Reading Panel as correlated with effective reading, encourages children to read extensively by themselves, both in and out of school, with little guidance or feedback. This approach will be discussed in Chapter 6.

THE VALUE OF REPEATED READINGS

One of the most efficient ways to improve children's oral reading fluency is through repeated readings (Samuels, 1979), in which children practice reading a passage or a short book three to five times, each time attempting to increase their reading rate while reducing the number of errors they make. To engage them in their own success, teachers can time the children's reading and plot their speed and accuracy; this way, children can see their improvements graphically. Children can also be given short comprehension assessments to ensure that fluency is not being increased without a concomitant increase in comprehension. Besides fostering increased reading fluency, repeated readings have been found to deepen comprehension of text (Yaden, 1988), as children revisit the material on successive sessions.

Samuels based the development of the repeated-readings process on disturbing practices he observed taking place during classroom reading instruction. Usually, children simply took turns reading aloud from their basal readers. When it came to their turn to read, many children were unable to do a "cold" reading with fluency and were often humiliated, as their classmates were forced to listen to them stumble through material at a plodding rate of speed. With only "one shot" at the material, many children experienced only failure on a daily basis and never had the opportunity to return to the material to try to improve their reading performance. Samuels theorized that this misguided instruction (also called *round robin reading*) should more closely align with the way other semi–skill-based fluencies are acquired, such as music. Most musicians, he mused, focus on one piece of music and practice it multiple times until it is smooth and polished. Then, feeling a sense of accomplishment, they move on to the next piece of music.

Instead of having children face new reading material on a daily basis, Samuels surmised that they might read the same passage multiple times until they have reached a predetermined level of fluency. He created a process whereby each child would read a passage aloud to an adult and then reread the passage silently several times. Then the child would again read the passage aloud to the adult. Only on reaching the designated reading rate for the passage would the child move on to a new passage, using the same procedure (Samuels, 2002). Although such practice did indeed increase reading rate, comprehension was often compromised when reading for meaning was not a part of the process and was not assessed.

REPEATED READING ACTIVITIES

Asking children to reread something they have just read must be done for an authentic purpose that can be explained to them; otherwise, it can be a boring, seemingly futile activity that can turn them off to reading as a pleasurable pursuit. Instead, children can be asked to rehearse a book or excerpt and then read it on tape, which will be donated to a local hospital for sick children and which students can use to evaluate their oral reading (see Exhibit 2.1). Or children can be asked to read a book aloud multiple times to prepare to be a fluent "guest reader" in a kindergarten class—always an appreciative audience! Repeated reading that takes place to prepare for a choral reading or readers theatre

exhibit 2.1 Self-evaluation of taped reading.

Did I:

- pronounce words correctly?
- read in phrases and thought units?
- pay attention to punctuation?
- read slowly enough for people to follow?
- read loudly enough so people could hear?
- convey the author's meaning to the audience?

performance, always an enjoyable and purposeful experience, will be addressed in the next two chapters. Other activities that provide students with an authentic purpose for repeated reading are provided below.

activity

Fluency Development Lesson

One procedure was created to provide fluency instruction especially for primary-age children who have been struggling with fluency (Rasinski, Padak, Linek, and Sturtevant, 1994). In the creators' lesson format, called the *fluency development lesson,* a procedure akin to echo reading involves the teacher reading aloud a section of text and the children repeating the section as they point to, or "track," the words they are reading. After hearing it read by the teacher, pairs of children have the opportunity to practice reading the passage with each other, thus adding an enjoyable social dimension to the lesson.

PREPARATION

Preparation for the lesson, which takes about 15 minutes of class time, requires the teacher to make copies of a 50–150 word text, one for each child. Though highly predictable and easy-to-read stories or poems are often used for this purpose, informational books, often of high interest to children, are also suitable For example, *What You Never Knew About Fingers, Forks, and Chopsticks* by Patricia Lauber (Simon & Schuster, 1999) provides a lesson in comparative cultures while informing children about the history of etiquette in a most interesting way. A list of other appropriate books for a fluency development lesson can be found in Appendix A.

PROCEDURE

Once the text is selected, the teacher follows these steps:

- Establish an authentic purpose for the multiple readings, such as preparing to read the passage at home to parents or caregivers.
- Read the passage aloud to the children while they use an index card to track the words in their own copies.
- Discuss the meaning of the passage with the children, as well as how it was read.
- Read the passage chorally with children, using a variety of formats (see Chapter 3), urging them to read it as you did.
- Divide the class into pairs and have children take turns reading the passage aloud three times, soliciting feedback and assistance, as necessary, from their partner.

- When the pairs are finished, ask for volunteers (individuals, pairs, or several pairs) to read the passage for the entire class, without help from the teacher.
- Using words chosen from the day's passage and previously read passages, initiate word play and create word banks and walls.
- Have children take the passage home and read it aloud to parents or caregivers.

Revised Radio Reading

This authentic approach to fluency development provides children with a highly motivational reason for repeatedly reading a passage—to become a radio announcer—and also offers the children who are assuming the role of "audience" a chance to listen critically in order to engage in subsequent discussion. (For more information, see Cecil, 2004.)

PREPARATION

Preparation for the lesson includes finding a short piece of literature from a basal reader or a trade book, written at the children's independent reading level. Such books can be fiction or nonfiction, but they should contain some measure of drama or excitement to offer children a reason to muster their best reading expression. (Suggestions: *The True and Terrifying Story of the Yellow Fever Epidemic of 1793* [Clarion Books, 2003], 4–6; *Biggest, Strongest, Fastest* by Steve Jenkins [Scholastic, 1995], 4–6; *Welcoming Babies* by Margie Burns Knight [Tilbury House, 1994], K–3; *Peppe the Lamplighter* by Elisa Bartone [Lothrop, Lee, & Shepard, 1993], K–3.)

PROCEDURE

- Divide the book into small numbered sections and give a section to each member of the group.
- Ask the children to rehearse their section by reading it out loud several times at school or to practice at home for a parent or caregiver.
- Model asking an open-ended question for one section of the book. For example, "What would *you* have done if the bully had taken *your* lunch?" Invite the children to create one such open-ended question for the section they have been assigned.
- Model reading a passage aloud, as a radio announcer might, while the children listen with their books closed. Then ask the child who has been assigned the first section of the book to read that passage as a radio announcer might.

activity

- Encourage the child to then ask his or her open-ended question about the section, leaving ample time for a discussion, should the question engage the other children.

- Have the other children in the group then read their sections in order, also adopting the persona of radio announcer, as the other children listen.

- Follow the reading of each section with the child's open-ended question and ensuing discussion.

POETRY AND FLUENCY

P oetry, read orally, is an ideal way to increase fluency in the elementary classroom. Because poetry by its very nature is meant to be read aloud for an audience, it is a terrific vehicle through which to promote fluent reading of intriguing text or original verse, which can be performed according to individual interpretation (Rasinski, 2000). Moreover, poetry is a universal language that can be made accessible to *all* children, regardless of primary language or ability level. When children write their own poetry, second-language learners can code-switch, or use words from English and their home language, to create an exotic and whimsical poem that they can share with their classmates.

I maintain that children should first write their own poetry, and then they can be introduced to the poetry of published authors. The writing of original poetry can motivate children to write prolifically, thus increasing their writing as well as their reading fluency. In this way, children will see themselves as "poets," and they will be less intimidated by the esoteric nature of some poetry or simply the quality of the poems of long-established poets (Cecil, 1994).

After they have written much poetry and shared it with classmates in a safe, nonjudgmental environment, they will be open to reading the poetry of published poets. Most children seem to be fascinated by the humorous poetry written by Shel Silverstein and Jack Prelutsky, but introducing children to many different poets and anthologies can allow children to discover their own interests. Some suggestions of suitable poetry anthologies may be found in Appendix A.

To ensure a performance that is exactly the way the child wants it creates an authentic reason for repeated readings of the chosen poem. Despite this capacity of poetry to offer purposeful reasons for the reading and rereading of engaging verse, it is often overlooked in the language arts curriculum (Perfect, 1999), perhaps because teachers themselves feel uncomfortable with poetry. If attention is focused on performance and not so much on critical analysis—which may have been the culprit in creating a residual disdain for poetry in many—poetry can be a powerful addition to an oral reading program designed to enhance fluency. Following are some activities that provide a way of introducing poetry in the classroom and increasing fluency at the same time.

Poem in My Pocket

Children can obtain valuable oral reading practice through an activity called "Poem in My Pocket."

PROCEDURE

- Invite children to select a poem for reading that they have composed themselves, or, after children have been introduced to many different poems and poets, invite them to write out one of their favorite poems.
- Then have them practice reading their poem several times until they can read it fluently. After the practice reading, have them place the poem in a pocket.
- At a specified time during the day, give a signal and have the children mill around the classroom asking each other, "What poem is in *your* pocket?"
- The other child responds by extracting the poem from his or her pocket and reading it aloud for the questioner, who may be another student, the teacher, or a visitor in the classroom.
- Then the poem reading is reciprocated.

Poetry Reconstruction

Another activity to develop fluency through poetry involves poetry reconstruction.

PREPARATION

To prepare for this activity, write out, on sturdy paper, a fairly lengthy poem or ballad (*The Wreck of the Hesperus* or *Annabel Lee* are two suggestions) with which the children are unfamiliar. Then cut the poem into strips that contain a few lines or phrases from the poem.

activity

activity

PROCEDURE

- Selecting a group of about 10 children, give each child two or three strips at random and tell them that their job is to read their lines several times and then work with the other children in the group to put the strips together to reconstruct the entire poem. Typically, with little guidance, children rise to the task by reading their strips aloud to the rest of the group.
- Have the children work together to organize the strips, rereading phrases in a variety of different orders. To accomplish this goal, children must attend to various orthographic and poetic conventions such as punctuation, syntax, rhyme, and semantics. As several phrases are pieced together in this manner, much repeated reading naturally occurs as children adjust and readjust the phrases until they are satisfied with their version.
- When they are finished, have them read the original to see how close they came to the author's poem (Yopp & Yopp, 2003).

Poetry Readings

The long-range goal of a poetry program must be to crown the poetry reading and writing with a celebratory program in which children read their poetry for an audience that may consist of just the class, other classes, or parents, or it can be housed in a library and be open to the community.

Poetry readings might take the form of weekly readings in an informal setting, using a portion of the classroom to create a coffee-house atmosphere, with a stool and microphone for the performer and the audience sitting cross-legged on the floor. By comparison, the celebratory program might take the form of a multimedia poetry reading, where children think of how their performance can be enhanced by appropriate lighting, background music, costumes, audience participation, puppets, dance, or any number of creative endeavors. Children can select their favorite poems, some they have written and others from their favorite poets, and spend considerable time in and out of class preparing and practicing their performances, increasing their reading fluency as they read the selections again and again to obtain just the right nuances. At the poetry-reading event, children then take turns performing their poems. Children may read some poems individually but may also choose to pair up with another child to create the possibility of different voices, or team up with two other children to add volume or intensity to the reading. Rasinski (2000) calls a version of this event a "Poetry Party" and describes one he observed where hot cider and popcorn were served to visitors and children's interpretive readings of the poems were met with hearty applause.

SINGING AND FLUENCY

Joyful singers of songs are learning more than just music. The whole child is involved. Children grow socially by learning to collaborate in the production of a song, and they grow emotionally through the opportunity to express and appreciate feelings in a powerful mode. The children develop coordination and control through such simple experiences as clapping or finger-snapping to a rhythm or moving to a beat. But children can also benefit tremendously from experience with repeated renditions of song lyrics. With appropriate guidance from the classroom teacher, children can extend their sight vocabulary, develop oral language, and increase their reading rate and accuracy (Cecil & Lauritzen, 1994). For children who have special language needs such as language delays, and for children with limited English or those who are learning English as a second language, songs—with their rhyme, rhythm, and repetition—are particularly potent paths to reading fluency (Jalongo & Bromley, 1984).

In one urban school in Sacramento, all the children begin the day in the Multipurpose Room, where they are led in a "community sing" by a teacher accompanying herself on the guitar. The teacher admits she knows only five chords and doesn't sing all that well, but no one seems to care. On the overhead projector, the lyrics of each song are prominently displayed for all to see. Joy is clearly evident on the faces of all children as they participate and practice the songs at their own level, with no pressure to demonstrate their skill (or lack thereof) as is required for solo singing. Copies of the songs sung during Community Sing are laminated and placed in classrooms and are frequently picked up during free-choice reading time.

Classroom Sing-Alongs

Singing need not be a whole school affair, as in the scenario from Sacramento. Teachers with limited musical ability, but with an interest in offering children another authentic, motivational reason for repeated reading, can conduct classroom sing-alongs by following the steps below.

PROCEDURE

- Select a song that is a familiar favorite of the children and that contains interesting words with rhyme, rhythm, and repetition to provide the best opportunity to practice fluent reading.

activity

- Link the words to print by writing the lyrics on a song chart. Lead the group in singing the song one phrase at a time and model strategies for encoding, or "sounding out," words by thinking out loud as the lyrics are written down.

- Invite the children to sing along once the chart is completed, and use a pointer to match each syllable of the words with a musical note to accentuate the rhythm of the song (the old "bouncing ball" of community singing).

- Use the chart to highlight repetitious words and phrases, and provide an opportunity to build sight vocabulary.

Some suggestions of commercial songbooks that are suitable for class sing-alongs can be found in Appendix A.

MODELING FLUENT READING

Children who have not developed proficient oral-reading skills are often unaware of what fluent reading should actually sound like (Rasinski & Padak, 2000). Often, with much round robin reading and other uninspired oral-reading practices occurring routinely in classrooms, children too frequently hear only models of disfluent readers who stumble over words and read painfully, laboriously, and slowly, without having had the opportunity to rehearse before reading aloud. Struggling readers and children for whom English is a second language, in particular, are often relegated for most of the day to groups of similar children who have limited oral-reading skills, and generally lack proficient models of fluent reading.

Teachers—at all grade levels—can do much to model fluent oral reading for children by reading aloud to them on a regular basis. Selecting material from a variety of genres, cultures, and writing styles, as well as including both informational text and fiction, can help children to understand the breadth of all that can be communicated in written form, as well as the appropriate pausing and expression needed for oral reading (Rasinski, 2003b). At the same time, English language learners become familiar with the rhythm and prosody of the English language by hearing excellent models of different types of writing being spoken.

Some of the modeling that the teacher does can be implicit, with children simply listening to the teacher and picking up her prosody through repeated exposure. But the teacher can also show children directly how to read with expression and pause according to the dictates of the author's punctuation. To do so, the teacher needs enough copies so that the children can be invited to read along. The teacher should exaggerate reading smoothly, making it "sound like talk," pausing appropriately for punctuation, and making sentences sound like questions (voice goes up), exclamations (words are louder), or statements (voice goes down). See Exhibit 2.2 for an example of a teacher modeling fluent reading.

After the teacher has demonstrated fluent reading, she should demonstrate a contrasting disfluent, monotonous reading of the same passage by reading word by word, omitting punctuation, and making every sentence sound exactly alike. Then the teacher can invite the children to make comparative comments about the two readings.

Another way to model fluent reading is to emphasize appropriate intonation, as in activities created by Blevins (2001). He suggests that the teacher use the alphabet broken up into several letter segments, followed by a variety of punctuation, to cue intonation (e.g., ABC! DEF? GHIJ. KLM? NOPQ. RST!). Similarly, Blevins proposes that modeling for children how to read the same sentence with differing word emphases can increase children's sensitivity to how word emphasis impacts meaning (e.g., I have found the gold. I *have* found the gold. I have *found* the gold. I have found the *gold.*).

Bringing in good recordings of texts being read also demonstrates the way written language can be read fluently, with proper pausing and intonation. Books on tape or CD with excellent narrators, such as Tony

exhibit 2.2 **Example of modeling fluent reading.**

(Teacher, reading:) "By and by, just before sundown, he started home to show his mother his beautiful pair of long red wings." *(Teacher says:)* Did you see how I grouped the words "By and by" and "just before sundown"? That's because those words go *together.* And then I paused just a bit before I read the words "he started home to show his mother his beautiful pair of long red wings." This comma *(teacher points to the comma)* that the author put in told me to do that.

(Teacher, reading another line:) "He said to his friend, 'Do you still want your red wings?' 'No, no!' said the Little Rabbit." *(Teacher says:)* Did you hear how my voice went up right here *(points to the question mark)?* That's because the rabbit was asking a question. And did you hear how my voice got louder and more excited right here *(points to the exclamation mark)?* That's because the author put in the exclamation mark to show *how* the Little Rabbit said those words.

Hillerman reading his exciting mysteries, offer children an opportunity to hear oral reading at its finest. Listening to recorded books may also create an alternative to listening to music on an iPod for children when riding in the car or otherwise spending their free time.

SUMMARY

Becoming a fluent reader is highly correlated with reading success, but not all children easily reach a level of rate, accuracy, and prosody that enables them to concentrate their energies on getting meaning from the printed page. To become fluent readers, children must be given many opportunities to practice oral reading themselves. Repeated readings offer children the needed practice to develop fluency and, not surprisingly, have been shown to have a positive effect on reading fluency. Fortunately, numerous instructional activities are now available that offer children authentic, engaging reasons to read a text multiple times. Several prototypical examples of such instructional activities have been highlighted in this chapter.

Some children lack models of fluent reading. They, as well as children for whom English is a second language, can benefit from listening to various kinds of text being read orally by a proficient reader who can demonstrate the nuances of expression, voice modulation, and proper adherence to punctuation. Many commercial recordings are available for this purpose, or children who are models of fluent reading can make recordings for other children to listen to.

The fact remains, however, that struggling readers are not likely to make significant gains in fluency, or in other areas of literacy, unless teachers find ways to encourage them to read eagerly on their own, both in and out of school, to ensure that they gain the abundant reading practice that can come only from wide reading. Chapter 6 addresses this concern.

REFERENCES

Blevins, W. (2001). *Building fluency: Lessons and strategies for reading success.* Scranton, PA: Scholastic.

Cecil, N. L. (1994). *For the love of language: Poetry for every learner.* Winnipeg, Manitoba: Portage & Main Press.

Cecil, N. L. (2004). *Activities for a comprehensive approach to literacy.* Scottsdale, AZ: Holcomb Hathaway.

Cecil, N. L., & Lauritzen, P. (1994). *Literacy and the arts for the integrated classroom: Alternative ways of knowing.* New York: Longman.

Jalongo, M. R., & Bromley, K. D. (1984). Developing linguistic competence through song picture books. *The Reading Teacher, 37,* 840–845.

National Reading Panel. (2000). *Report of the National Reading Panel: Teaching children to read: An evidence-based assessment of the scientific research literature on reading and its implications for reading instruction.* Washington, DC: National Institute of Child Health and Human Development, National Institutes of Health.

Osborn, J., & Lehr, F. (2000). *A focus on fluency.* Honolulu, HI: Regional Educational Laboratory at Pacific Resources for Education and Learning.

Perfect, K. A. (1999). Rhyme and reason: Poetry for the heart and head. *The Reading Teacher, 52,* 728–737.

Rasinski, T. V. (2000). Speed does matter in reading. *The Reading Teacher, 54,* 146–151.

Rasinski, T. V. (2003a). Beyond speed: Reading fluency is more than reading fast. *The California Reader, 2,* 5–11.

Rasinski, T. V. (2003b). *The fluent reader: Oral reading strategies for building word recognition, fluency, and comprehension.* New York: Scholastic.

Rasinski, T., & Padak, N. (2000). *Effective reading strategies: Teaching children who find reading difficult.* Upper Saddle River, NJ: Merrill Prentice Hall.

Rasinski, T. V., Padak, N., Linek, W. L., & Sturtevant, E. (1994). Effects of fluency development on urban second-grade readers. *Journal of Educational Research, 87,* 158–165.

Samuels, S. J. (1979). The method of repeated readings. *The Reading Teacher, 32,* 403–408.

Samuels, S. J. (2002). Reading fluency: Its development and assessment. In A. E. Farstrup & S. J. Samuels (Eds.), *What research has to say about reading instruction* (3rd ed., pp. 166–183). Newark, DE: International Reading Association.

Yaden, D. B., Jr. (1988). Understanding stories through repeated read-alouds: How many does it take? *The Reading Teacher, 41,* 556–560.

Yopp, R. H., & Yopp, H. K. (2003). Time with text. *The Reading Teacher, 57,* 284–287.

Choral Reading and Fluency | 3

Choral reading is certainly not a new activity, as its origins can be traced back to early Greek drama and to tribal chants used in religious and other ceremonies. So what is it doing in a book concerned with reading fluency?

The sheer enjoyment that children experience when they are participating in a carefully chosen choral reading piece justifies that it should hold a prominent place in the K–6 literacy curriculum. Most children, after honing a piece of choral reading to perfection, want to perform it again and again, in front of as many audiences as they can find. But choral reading has other, unique qualities that make it a necessary part of any literacy curriculum: Children who get satisfaction from expressing themselves vocally, but who are too shy to speak in front of the class by themselves, find that they lose their self-consciousness when performing in a sea of other speakers. Similarly, children for whom English is a second language feel safe performing with others, and they also find themselves picking up the tones, rhythm, and cadence of English as they simultaneously read words that their classmates are speaking all around them. Finally, Homan, Klesius, and Hite (1993) conclude that choral reading, when using such arrangements as echoic and unison readings, yields significant gains in fluency and comprehension for all children. Simply stated, choral reading is ideal fluency practice that is carried out in a most motivational and authentic way.

For the purpose of fluency development, choral reading is invaluable in the elementary classroom as a flexible activity with many different uses. Choral reading can involve soloists, or several or many children simultaneously reading the same material aloud, and it can be seamlessly integrated into many other parts of the literacy curriculum. Children can chorally read verse and poems as part of literature focus units, thematic units, or reader's workshop. With props and simple costumes, they may perform the readings for other classes, back-to-school nights, or other evening performances. Choral reading can be the foundation for an art, music, or drama lesson as children find creative ways to present their reading with multimedia.

Choral reading provides ample repeated-reading practice, so necessary to the enhancement of fluency as discussed in Chapter 2, without the usual monotony. After selecting an appropriate piece, the teacher initially models the fluent reading of the text for the children and then the children read it—and reread it—together, until they are all satisfied that they have read it in a fluent, natural, and pleasing manner (Yopp & Yopp, 2003). The necessary repeated readings lead to increased fluency. But while many other instructional strategies designed to foster fluency attend mostly to the components of rate and accuracy, few strategies attend to prosody, or the appropriate reading expression that makes the reading somehow sound "natural." Choral reading increases prosody by allowing children to practice reading with the same expression, natural pauses, and tone of voice that the teacher has displayed.

HOW TO INITIATE A CHORAL READING

Initiating a choral reading program is relatively simple and cost-effective. It requires finding reading material that does the following:

- Meets the children's independent reading level
- Is fun to read aloud
- Contains a mood or an emotion (scary, sad, funny, thoughtful, awe-inspiring, and so forth)
- Has special sound features (alliteration, silly words, or amusing rhymes)

The chosen material can be poetry or verse, or even ritual material such as *The Gettysburg Address*. It must be enjoyable to read to an audience and be easily divisible among class members so that all have the chance to participate.

To ensure that children do not regress into a monotonous, sing-song recitation after multiple readings of the same piece, the teacher must keep the repetitions fresh. There will be a strong tendency toward sameness in the effect of reading pieces of verse in chorus unless the teacher clearly appreciates poetry and verse and carefully collaborates with the class to consider possible ways to interpret each piece of writing. The teacher must help the children visualize the word pictures and images that the writing evokes. When children have these images clearly in mind, they will speak in a more natural, un-self-conscious way. Optimally, a group of children performing a choral reading will be imbued with a desire to make the pieces of writing come alive for others by firing their imagination with the thoughts conveyed, whether those thoughts are of strength, beauty, fear, or laughter.

Sometimes, the teacher may observe that certain children are having difficulty keeping up with the speaking tempo of the group. Other times, some children may need additional help discerning the proper dynamics of the piece, or they may simply be having problems pronouncing some of the words. In such cases, the teacher may empower these students by allowing them to serve as "the audience," with specific instructions to listen carefully to the other speakers and consider some suggestions to make the reading more effective. When the children acting as the audience rejoin the group, they usually do so with added zest and confidence, and a clearer understanding of the nature of the choral reading selection; moreover, this strategy often brings forth suggestions from the listeners that are helpful to the future success of the reading performance.

activity

Creating a Choral Reading

The following steps can be used to create a choral reading performance with children (Tompkins, 1998):

PROCEDURE

- Select a poem or verse that is at the children's independent reading level. See Appendix A for suggestions.
- Copy it onto a chart or overhead transparency, or make a copy for each child.
- Read the piece to the children with the expression, tempo, and intonation you want them to emulate, while they follow along in the text.
- Brainstorm with the children about how the piece might be divided for multigroup reading. Mark these ideas in the text.
- Read the piece, with the children joining in, several times at a natural speed, enunciating each word carefully. (For the benefit of second language learners, it is sometimes helpful to stand so that these learners can watch how the teacher's mouth forms the words.)
- Guide the children as they read the piece in the agreed-upon groups. Stress proper pronunciation of words, expression, and appropriate speed and volume.
- Optionally, tape-record or videotape the reading so that the children can listen to their own voices and follow along, possibly deciding also if it is necessary to rearrange the voices in the choral reading.

TEACHING TYPOGRAPHICAL CUES

The use of choral reading provides an excellent opportunity to teach children how punctuation informs readers when to make small adjustments in their reading. For example, a comma signals that the reader must take a short pause, and text in capital letters usually signals an increase in volume, while a question mark at the end of a sentence requires the reader to adjust the intonation (see Exhibit 3.1). Understanding these typographical cues helps children to reconstruct the text, with all its innuendos, exactly as it is intended to be read, thus increasing their comprehension.

exhibit 3.1 **Typographical signals and what they stand for.**

SIGNAL	WHAT IT MEANS	EXAMPLE
Comma	Need for pause; placement affects meaning	Nan, my dog, is as cute as you. Nan, my dog is as cute as you.
Period	Need a longer pause	The sky looked mysterious.
Question mark	Intonation at end of sentence	Will you really?
Exclamation mark	Need to read with emotion	That's terrific!
Underlined, enlarged, or bold print	Need for stress	He's a <u>fabulous</u> cook! **He's** a fabulous cook!
Combination	Shows special stress	The student sighed, "I am <u>SO</u> bored with this class!"

Source: Adapted with permission from *Good-bye Round Robin: 25 Effective Oral Reading Strategies* by Michael F. Opitz and Timothy Rasinski. Copyright © 1998 by Michael F. Opitz and Timothy Rasinski. Published by Heinemann, a division of Reed Elsevier, Inc., Portsmouth, NH. All rights reserved.

Mini-Lesson on Typographical Cues

Understanding the subtleties of punctuation can further children's fluency by increasing their understanding of the author's intended expression, or prosody. This mini-lesson can be used to help children become aware of the importance of typographical cues for the purpose of enhancing their ability to perform choral reading fluently (adapted from Opitz & Rasinski, 1998).

activity

PROCEDURE

- Create a mini-lesson for each typographical cue. Using the signals from Exhibit 3.1, find a sentence within a choral reading piece that contains specific examples of one of these signals, such as the use of question marks.
- Put the choral reading passage on chart paper or on the overhead projector so all children can see.
- Tell children you will read each sentence twice and you want them to decide which reading is more effective or interesting. For the first

reading, use a monotone voice and ignore the typographical cues; for the second reading, follow the cues and read with appropriate expression. For example, first read:

"Was that you making all that noise. I thought it was a herd of elephants."

Then read:

"Was that _you_ making all that noise? I thought it was a herd of elephants!"

- Ask children: Which reading was more interesting? Did following the signals help them understand what the author was trying to convey? Finally, call attention to the specific typographical cues and how they help to clarify the author's meaning.
- Have children search for reading material in the room that contains examples of the typographical cue that was discussed. Invite them to read the sentence aloud and describe, in their own words, what they think the signal is telling them to do.

FIVE CHORAL READING FORMATS

When performing choral reading with children, the basic approach is to have all children read in unison. This approach provides excellent practice in fluency as well as in the pronunciation and cadence of the English language for those for whom English is a second language. However, having all children read all of the reading at the same time can get tiresome. The different voices contained in the reading can sometimes be divided up for a change of pace.

Five basic arrangements are used when dividing up the voices for choral reading. Using varied formats helps to keep motivation high, and children will soon see for themselves that certain passages are more suited to one arrangement than another, as we will discuss in this section. Also, with experience, children will be willing and able to contribute some original ideas for other innovative speaking formats that best correspond to the composition of the children in the class.

Unison Reading

The simplest arrangement for use in choral reading is _unison reading,_ in which all the children in the class speak all of the lines together at the same time. Tempo, volume, rhythm, and intonation may vary but all children will make the variations at once. Such a straightforward arrangement is a good way to begin the activity of choral reading, especially if some children are reluctant speakers or second language learners who are just beginning to feel comfortable speaking in English. Unison reading is also appropriate with ritual text, such as *The Gettysburg Address,* that may require little change in tonal quality. Following is an example of a verse appropriate for unison reading.

WAVES

(softly)

I'd like to be a wave,

A little rolling wave,

A wave that gently laps along the beach.

(A bit louder)

I'd like to be a wave,

A naughty, careless wave,

That throws toy sailboats out of reach.

(triumphantly)

I'd like to be a wave

A CRASHING, SMASHING wave!

A wave that tumbles ships at sea!

(softly)

I guess I'd like to be a wave,

I'd like to be just ANY wave,

For every wave, it seems, is free!

—N. L. CECIL

Echoic Reading

A second arrangement for choral reading that is also helpful to second language speakers is *echoic reading.* This is a true imitative method that requires the teacher to read each line, and then all the children to repeat it immediately afterwards. This method has the advantage of allowing the teacher to continue to model the pronunciation of each word, the tonal qualities, the tempo and volume, and the exact expression that is needed in each line, ensuring increased fluency much more quickly than in each of the other choral reading arrangements. Echoic reading works best when the selection has some repetitive parts that become even stronger with the added repetitions the children provide. For example:

THE DRUM

I bought a little drum. *(children repeat)*

Ta-tum, ta-tum! *(children repeat)*

I beat the little drum. *(children repeat)*

Ta-tum, ta-tum! *(children repeat)*

"Let's march," said the drum! *(children repeat)*

Ta-tum, ta-tum! *(children repeat)*

"All right, Little Drum!" *(children repeat)*

Ta-tum, ta-tum! *(children repeat)*

I had SO much fun . . . *(children repeat)*

Ta-tum, ta-tum! *(children repeat)*

Marching with my drum! *(children repeat)*

Ta-tum, ta-tum! *(children repeat)*

—ANONYMOUS

Verse and Refrain Reading

The most common arrangement for choral reading is known as *verse and refrain reading*. In this format, a soloist or small group of readers is given the opportunity to read the verse, or the main part of the poem, and the rest of the class reads the refrain, or chorus, together. This arrangement is especially suitable when the teacher wants to highlight a certain student or students who are in need of fluency practice and who can become the refrain speaker(s), although different soloists can perform in the same choral reading if the teacher so desires. This format is also especially appropriate when the chosen material has a clearly defined, repetitive refrain, as in the following example.

THE FROG'S SONG

Soloist(s):   You'll know when it really is Springtime

You'll be sure that it's really begun,

When the frogs that live down in the meadow,

Wake up and . . .

Chorus: . . . croak, "Jump and run! Jump and run!"

Soloist(s):   Grandfather frog has been sleeping

In the mud, far away from the sun.

Now he hip hops to the edge of the pond

Chorus:	. . . And he croaks, "Jump and run! Jump and run!"
Soloist(s):	Such a commotion you never have heard,
	For no frog wants his singing outdone.
	Each swells up with pride, and from deep down inside
Chorus:	. . . Comes that croak, "Jump and run! Jump and run!"

—TRADITIONAL

Cumulative Reading

A fourth arrangement for choral reading is called *cumulative reading*. With this method, one reader begins by reading the first line of the piece, and then one after another reader joins in until each line in the piece has been read. Because the accumulation of voices in this arrangement naturally causes the reading to become increasingly greater in volume, this method of choral reading is especially effective when the desired effect is a building of intensity. An added bonus is that children must follow along with the reading to listen carefully for their cue to begin. A rereading of the same selection may begin with a new leader and children joining in a different order. For example:

THE SNOWFLAKES ARE FALLING

Everyone:	The snowflakes are falling!
	The snowflakes are falling!
Leader:	I wonder if they'll stay?
Everyone:	(repeat first two lines, softly)
Add a reader:	I hope they don't melt away.
Everyone:	(repeat first two lines, softly)
Add a reader:	One landed on my nose.
Everyone:	(repeat first two lines, getting louder)
Add a reader:	Now they cover my toes!
Everyone:	(repeat first two lines, getting louder)
Add a reader:	I see them in the trees . . .
Everyone:	(repeat first two lines, getting louder)
Add a reader:	Now they're up to my knees!
Everyone:	(repeat the first two lines, getting louder)
Add a reader:	I stick out my tongue for a taste . . .
Everyone:	(repeat the first two lines, getting louder)

Add a reader:	Now they're up to my waist!
Everyone:	(repeat the first two lines, loudly)
Add a reader:	Each one's a special guest.
Everyone:	(repeat the first two lines, loudly)
Add a reader:	Now they're up to my chest!
Everyone:	(repeat the first two lines, loudly)
Add a reader:	Covering cities and farms . . .
Everyone:	(repeat the first two lines, loudly)
Add a reader:	Now they cover my arms!
Everyone:	(repeat the first two lines, louder)
Add a reader:	Each a contest could win . . .
Everyone:	(repeat the first two lines, louder)
Add a reader:	Oh, dear, OH DEAR! They're up to my CHIN!
Everyone:	(repeat the first two lines, more loudly)
Add a reader:	Falling like baby's tears . . .
Everyone:	(repeat the first two lines, loudly)
Add a reader:	Yikes! They cover my EARS!
Everyone:	(repeat the first two lines, more loudly)
Add a reader:	Soon they'll cover my HEAD!
Everyone:	(repeat the first two lines, much more loudly)
The leader, alone:	OOPS! I'm only dreaming in bed!
Chorus: (softly)	The snowflakes are falling!
	The snowflakes are falling!

—AUTHOR UNKNOWN

Antiphonal Reading

Antiphonal reading features one set of voices answering another set of voices, with each set perhaps having a different pitch or tonal quality. Two discrete divisions in a poem or verse may make it ideal for this choral reading format. Paul Fleishman (see the listing of books for poetry and choral reading in Appendix A) has written several books with poems selected specifically for this kind of reading, already arranged for the two groups. To vary this format, the class can be divided not into two groups but into as many groups as the class's interpretation of the poem permits. This arrangement is enjoyable when two very different pitches or tonal qualities are needed to highlight the contrast in the mood of the selection, such as higher voices for sunny moods and lower voices for sad moods. In the following example, high voices ask questions, as the voice at the end of a question goes up in pitch, while the low voices provide the answers, as one's pitch goes down in the end to an answer.

WHAT'S IN THERE?

Group one (high voices):	Group two (low voices):
What's in there?	Gold and money.
Where's my share of it?	The mouse ran away with it.
Where's the mouse?	In her house.
Where's her house?	In the woods.
Where's the woods?	The fire burned them.
Where's the fire?	The water quenched it.
Where's the water?	The scary bull drank it.
Where's the scary bull?	In back of the hill.
Where's the hill?	Covered with snow.
Where's the snow?	The sun melted it.
Where's the sun?	High up in the air.
Is this the end?	We don't care!

—AUTHOR UNKNOWN

ESPECIALLY FOR EARLY READERS

Early readers and second language learners who are just beginning to crack the code of our language can benefit greatly from choral reading, especially when the selections chosen focus on a certain phonemic element that the class is studying. A basic sight vocabulary is also built through the use of this approach. While the children follow along, the teacher should first read the piece, pointing out the pronunciation of unfamiliar words, and then help the children to discover the pattern that is created by the particular phonemic element. For example, if children are working on beginning sounds, an alliterative poem such as the following would be appropriate to read in unison, or using echoic reading:

THE SWAN'S SONG

Swan swam over the sea.

Swim, swan, swim!

Swan swam back again.

Well swum, swan!

—*TRADITIONAL*

If children are working on rhyming, or ending sounds, many effective, short rhyming poems are available that children could read several times to reinforce these concepts. For example,

THE ZANY ZOO

Granny, Granny, come to the zoo!

A monkey has swallowed a kangaroo!

A lion is chasing a circus clown,

And the tigers are pacing upside down!

The turtles are taking the bears for a ride,

And the zebras are climbing on a slippery slide!

They're sliding down the tall giraffe,

You have to see this, Granny!

It will make you LAUGH!

—*N. L. CECIL*

MULTIMEDIA EXTENSIONS

To add interest and curricular integration to choral reading, the class can decide on some appropriate multimedia extensions to enhance the feeling or mood of the selection. Moreover, for those children who express themselves best through art, drama, or music, adding these activities offers another enjoyable dimension. At the same time, the multisensory facets of art, drama, and music add comprehensible input that reinforces the meaning of the choral reading selection for the benefit of children for whom English is a second language.

Art

To add art to the choral reading, children might create puppets to act out the events as they are being read. Original photographs could be used in the background to underscore the characters in a selection. Children can also create colorful costumes to wear while doing the choral performances, or wear body paint or face make-up to create a mood. Finally, all children will enjoy designing interesting props that could be used at appropriate times during the reading.

Drama

Drama can make a choral reading come to life and add excitement. Simply having children take a dramatic step forward, fold their arms, or turn around as they are the answering voices adds interest to a performance. Also, dimming the lights or using candles, or scents such as incense or potpourri, can create a desired mood. Younger children enjoy making actions that accompany the words, such as forming a sun with their arms, yawning, or pretending to rock a baby. The audience might be asked, through the use of cue cards, to laugh at certain times ("Ha ha!") or to express disgust with a line from the selection ("Boo!"). Also, children can use an innovative technique called "performance art" in which they ask the audience to participate in the choral reading in any way that seems appropriate. For example, the audience might be given small hand mirrors and asked to look into them during a choral reading about introspection; or the audience might be asked to extend their arms high in the air, to "reach for the sky," during a reading about achievement. Finally, a choral reading that is frightening or very intense in nature can be made more so by adding special sound effects (a creaking door, howling wind, thunder, and so forth) as well as appropriate lighting.

Music

Music can be used to invoke the mood that is intended by the choral reading. By selecting several classical musical selections, such as Edvard Grieg's *Peer Gynt Suite,* and playing them for children when they are between activities or before school has begun, teachers will help children become familiar with a repertoire of music that they can choose to enhance their choral reading. Also, simple musical instruments, such as maracas, tambourines, or drums, are wonderful accompaniments to choral reading, when the action or mood lends itself to such additions. For example, one third-grade class did a choral reading of *The Song of Hiawatha* that was made considerably more memorable by the soft beating of drums.

SUMMARY

Choral reading is an ideal way to make repeated readings, which are so important for increasing fluency, both enjoyable and authentic. Fortunately, choral reading is very easy to institute in the classroom. The process requires only selecting interesting poems or verses and then deciding how best to arrange the group so that all children have an opportunity to speak. The chapter offered five different ways to format a choral reading selection, but with experience children can create many other innovative ways to arrange a reading.

Teachers are urged to maintain the interest in and motivation for choral reading by using multimedia extensions to make each choral reading come to life. Art, drama, and music can all be used to enhance the reading and make it truly come to life. After all, the goal of choral reading, besides increasing fluency in an authentic way, is to communicate an author's message through personal expression. Although that expression begins in spoken form, it only becomes richer when other senses are added to the reading.

Finally, choral reading is an excellent way to allow all children in a class to become fluent in an enjoyable yet totally nonthreatening way. Because the selection is performed as a group, cooperation and teamwork are paramount. Moreover, second language learners receive invaluable practice reading and speaking words with abundant modeling of appropriate expression and pronunciation. And for those children who may be a bit hesitant to perform on their own or even to read aloud in front of other children, the support from the rest of the group allows them to have a successful oral reading experience. And as all educators know well, success can only breed success.

REFERENCES

Fleishman, P. (1988). *Joyful noise: Poems for two voices.* New York: Harper & Row.

Fleishman, P. (2000). *Big talk: Poems for four voices.* Cambridge, MA: Candlewick.

Cecil, N. L. (1994). *For the love of language: Poetry for every learner.* Winnipeg, Manitoba: Portage and Main Press.

Graves, D. H. (1992). *Explore poetry.* Portsmouth, NH: Heinemann.

Homan, S. P., Klesius, J. P., & Hite, C. (1993). Effects of repeated readings and nonrepetitive strategies on students' fluency and comprehension. *The Journal of Educational Research, 87,* 94–99.

Hull, D. (1994). *I am the dog/I am the cat.* New York: Dial.

Larrick, N. *Let's do a poem! Introducing poetry to children.* New York: Delacorte Press.

Opitz, M. F., & Rasinski, T. V. (1998). *Good-bye round robin: 25 effective oral reading strategies.* Portsmouth, NH: Heinemann.

Tompkins, G. E. (1998). *50 literacy strategies: Step by step.* Upper Saddle River, NJ: Merrill.

Yopp, R. H., & Yopp, H. K. (2003). Time with text. *The Reading Teacher, 57,* 284–287.

Drama and Fluency 4

A s far back as most people can remember, children have been acting in school plays, dressing up as carrots or bunnies or angels and appearing on stages in stuffy auditoriums. Often, the children forget their lines, or are unable to be heard beyond the second row, but everyone involved is delighted anyway. They think something special and wonderful is happening, and they are exactly right.

The inherent value of dramatic experiences for children, in general, has been cited by many proponents of this unique art form. Moreover, Edmiston, Encisco, and King (1987) insist that drama should be at the very core of language development and learning. Indeed, drama, more than most other art forms, has held a place of honor in many language arts curricula because creative teachers intuitively know that through drama (yes, even in the above scenarios) children are increasing fluency as they read and reread for the authentic purpose of familiarizing themselves with or memorizing scripts, while language development and collaborative skills also increase. Moreover, the value of drama for those children for whom English is a second language is priceless. When children act out a scene, an event, or a favorite story, they are providing a comprehensible context for the concomitant words and are offering English language learners, in my opinion, the highest form of language development in the most enjoyable way.

A committee sponsored by the National Endowment for the Arts elaborated on the value of drama, suggesting the following:

- Drama offers a creative and psychological balance to more routine academic instruction.
- Drama offers children a "magical" experience that contains an alternative way to view reality.
- Drama is respectful of childhood in that it showcases a sense of pretending and wonder.
- Drama enhances ability in all other academic areas by making children better thinkers (Corathers, 1991).

Several specific types of drama offer children an exciting break from their regular routine and are also ideally suited to increase fluency in a highly motivational way while providing a visual context in which children, especially those learning English, can increase their language prowess (Tyler & Chard, 2000). These specific types of drama are commercial plays, readers theatre and improvised sketches from favorite stories, and original dramatic pieces. Each of these will be discussed at length in the remainder of this chapter.

READING COMMERCIAL PLAYS

A powerful way to introduce children to the conventions of play writing while increasing fluency is by allowing them to read commercially prepared plays. Plays appropriate for a wide range of grade levels are readily available in booklets that can be found in most elementary libraries, including some excellent resources such as

The Playwright's Corner. The following collections are some examples offering reproducible scripts:

- *25 Just-Right Plays for Emergent Readers* (Pugliano-Martin, 1998) includes simple plays for beginning readers.

- *Easy-to-Read Folk and Fairy Tale Plays* (Pugliano, 1999) offers a selection of seven plays for first- and second-grade readers.

- *Tall Tales Read-Aloud Plays* (Pugliano-Martin, 2000) is a collection of eight adaptations of traditional stories that may be integrated with social studies, math, and language arts in the third through fifth grades.

- *Revolutionary War Read-Aloud Plays* (Murphy, 2000) is a collection of five plays set during the American Revolution and appropriate for children in the fourth through eighth grades.

Grade-appropriate plays can also be found in many basal readers as well as some trade books.

Before doing a full-blown dramatic production, children must possess certain understandings. Most critically, reading plays is quite different from reading the ordinary narrative and expository material to which children are normally exposed. Because plays are mainly concerned with dialogue, they focus children's attention on the natural conversations that are an integral part of their lives. Thus, reading plays can help children graphically experience the relationship between print and spoken language. A play's script allows children to understand the textual details of a story and fosters basic language skills as well as interpretive reading. Discussion about the way the dialogue should be delivered helps children, especially English language learners, to become sensitive to differing language styles and usage that fits the context and the characters. For example, a teacher might engage children in a discussion of similar characters with whom they are familiar, or experiences they have had, to help them understand how a character might talk and behave: "How do you think Scooby Doo would say this?" or "How might you say this line if you were telling someone they had just won a trip to Disneyland?" or "Pretend your mother just punished you by taking away television privileges for a week. Act out how you would feel while you are speaking these lines" (Cecil & Lauritzen, 1994).

The first reading of a play should begin with the teacher explaining the particular conventions of scripts; for example, that the name of the character is followed by a colon, a required action is indicated by parentheses, and so forth. The teacher can initially model fluent reading of the play. Subsequently, the teacher might assign roles to various children and conduct a "cold" reading. After that, a discussion can ensue that will focus on honing in on the specific inflections that each character might use, as well as alternate interpretations for the reading of certain lines. This discussion would be followed by a second reading, with revisions based on the discussion. Subsequent readings can follow with children switching roles. In this way, the more proficient readers provide some modeling for the less fluent readers.

When children have read several plays in this manner, they are ready to begin to use the dialogue in their favorite stories to create their own readers theatre script.

PERFORMING READERS THEATRE

Readers theatre is a group oral-reading strategy that allows children to practice reading from a script and then share their perfected reading with an audience of classmates, other grade levels, or adults (Allington, 2001). Unlike a more formal dramatic production, children need not memorize lines or use extensive props or stage sets for the presentation. The success of the readers theatre production depends on the oral aspects of the production rather than on acting skills or grand props, costumes, and make-up. The focus, instead, is on presenting an oral interpretation of the literature for the audience, who must use their imaginations to visualize the setting and action. Above all, readers theatre provides children with an authentic reason to read and reread a script several times. Because the reading culminates in an actual performance, children's motivation tends to be high and, therefore, they willingly engage in the many necessary rehearsals, all of which results naturally in increased reading fluency.

The motivational teaching strategy of readers theatre also has the benefit of allowing the teacher to model reading fluency before the children prepare to perform for an audience, showing them how the emphasis is now on communicating through the emotions that can be conveyed through oral reading. Perhaps because of this modeling, as well as the rereading afforded, readers theatre has been found to increase the fluency of different levels of readers, including average (Martinez, Roser, & Strecker, 1999) and low-performing readers (Millin & Rinehart, 1999; Rinehart, 1999). Likewise, Rasinski (1999) found that students who engaged in readers theatre made more than twice the gains in reading rate than those students provided with more traditional reading experiences. While children work collaboratively with their peers and prepare to read the script for an audience, rereading occurs as an authentic by-product.

Readers theatre can play an especially significant part in increasing fluency when it is an integral part of a comprehensive literacy program. For example, in one instance where readers theatre was used experimentally as a the main focus of the literacy program, researchers met with two classes of second-grade children for half an hour a day for 10 weeks (Martinez, Roser, & Strecker, 1999). On the first day of each week, the teachers read aloud the story on which the script was based and then conducted a brief lesson on some aspect of fluency, such as phrasing or reading with expression. Children were then given their own scripts to read and reread independently. On the following two days, children convened in small collaborative groups, where they read the script together several times, taking different roles with each subsequent reading. At the end of the session on the third day, children chose their roles for the performance. On the next day, children practiced the roles they selected with their groups, and on the final day they performed the readers theatre selection for the rest of the class or for another audience. The researchers found that significant gains in reading rate were achieved for some of the children after participating in this intensive readers theatre program (Yopp & Yopp, 2003).

Readers theatre differs from reading commercial scripts mainly in that usually the children, with guidance from the teacher, revise familiar literature, turning it into scripts. They do this by separating the dialogue from the action and descriptive parts of a favorite piece of literature. One or more narrators are assigned to "tell" the other parts of the story, while the characters in the story read the dialogue as it was originally put forth. Optionally, children can be encouraged to create a new script by paraphrasing the words of the characters and thus penning their own version of the piece of literature. Another variation, as discussed in the next section, is to use content area material as a source for readers theatre scripts.

Selecting Literature for Scripts

Literature chosen for readers theatre should be drawn from tales originating from the oral tradition, poetry, or high-quality picture books suitable to be read aloud by children. Stories selected should be action-filled, suspenseful, and made up of an entire self-contained episode. The literature chosen should require a minimum of rewriting, or a prepared readers theatre script can be used. The kind of story that is best adapted for readers theatre contains characters who have multidimensional features and unique personalities. The language of such a story should be thought provoking, colorful, and rhythmic. Ideally, the plot should have an element of conflict or suspense. Books such as *The Ant and the Elephant,* by Bill Peets (Atheneum, 1975) and *Alexander and the Terrible, Horrible, No Good, Very Bad Day,* by Judith Viorst (Atheneum, 1972) are good examples. Folktales are especially well-suited to the vehicle. A list of other books that are easily adaptable to readers theatre is offered by Worthy and Broaddus (2001/2002).

Others (e.g., Young & Vardell, 1993) have suggested that nonfiction material—including biography and informational literature—is also suitable for readers theatre. Adapting biography for readers theatre might mean having children who have had experiences with the subject of the biography tell the subject's story in their own voices. Content material in social studies and science also lends itself to readers theatre productions. For example, a script for the first Thanksgiving could be easily prepared, or children could think of inventive ways to present information about the rainforest from the perspective of its plants and/or animals. Teachers who think of content material as source material for readers theatre will be helping children become more fluent while they are also learning content in a motivational fashion. One resource that brings together science and biography in readers theatre scripts is Kendall Haven's *Great Moments in Science: Experiments and Readers Theatre* (1996). In each chapter, the author provides background on a topic such as Benjamin Franklin's discovery of electricity. The information is then followed by a script to help bring the information to life. In addition to the scripts, the book includes instructions for conducting related experiments that enable the students to "act" as scientists. According to Kane (2007), "the figures in the book may pass along their intellectual curiosity to those portraying them and those watching the skits, which show how the scientists engaged in critical thinking, overcame natural and political problems, and made connections among data and disciplines" (p. 255).

Whether the literature selected is fiction or nonfiction, it should have or provide ideas for enough dialogue to involve most of the children in the class. Any sections that don't include conversation can become narrator parts. Depending on the number of narrator lines, one to four children may share the narrator duties. The teacher may choose to photocopy the book for children to highlight as they develop the script. These marked-up copies can be used as the finished script, or the teacher (or children) may choose to retype the finished script in script format, leaving out any unnecessary parts (Tompkins, 1998). The completed script may be made into a laminated booklet and placed in a learning center for children to enjoy later as a free-time oral-reading activity.

Although most readers theatre, by definition, evolves from literature and involves children culling the dialogue they wish to choose from the story, some readers theatre scripts are available commercially, in which the dialogue is already excerpted and ready for the children to read. A list of such ready-made readers theatre scripts can be found in Appendix A or online at www.aaronshop.com/rt/.

Exhibit 4.1 shows the first page of a script for *The Boy Who Cried Wolf*, created by a class of third-grade students.

exhibit 4.1 Sample script page.

CAST OF CHARACTERS

Narrator 1	Shepherd Boy/Girl	Wolf	Sheep 1	Villager 1
Narrator 2	Mother	Sage 1	Sheep 2	Villager 2
Narrator 3	Father	Sage 2	Sheep 3	Villager 3
Narrator 4	Sheep dog	Sage 3		

NARRATOR 1: Once upon a time a young shepherd boy lived in a hillside village with his mother, his father, and his faithful sheep dog, Shep. Every morning he would herd his sheep into the hills, with good old Shep by his side.

MOTHER: Good bye, dear! Have a great day, and don't forget the yummy lunch I made for you!

FATHER: And be careful not to stray too far. I hear there have been some wolf sightings recently.

SHEPHERD: Oh, Mom and Dad, you know nothing ever happens up there. It's really *boring!* C'mon, Shep, Let's go! Bye, guys!

NARRATOR 2: So the shepherd made his way to the hillside with his dog, Shep, by his side and the sheep following him, making gentle sheep noises. He soon became bored and decided to have some fun.

SHEPHERD: I know what! I'll pretend I see a wolf and call the villagers! Maybe they'll spend some time with me so I won't be so lonely!

NARRATOR 3: So the boy cried out in a loud, scared voice . . .

SHEPHERD: Wolf! WOLF!!

NARRATOR 4: And some villagers left their work and came running up the hillside to see what the trouble was.

VILLAGER 1: *(Huffing and puffing)* Shepherd Boy! Shepherd Boy! Whatever is the matter?

VILLAGER 2: *(Huffing and puffing)* Did you see a wolf?

VILLAGER 3: *(Huffing and puffing)* So, where *is* this wolf?

NARRATOR 1: The villagers, seeing that there was no wolf, quickly returned to their work in the village. The shepherd boy went back to tending his sheep. But soon he began to become bored again.

Adaptations

An adaptation of readers theatre that is especially suited for English language learners is "books on tape," which are literature selections recorded for an unseen audience. Using this method, small groups of children select a piece of quality literature, create a script, and practice reading it until it becomes fluent and expressive, adding sound effects where appropriate, and including various voices for different characters. One teacher in Sowams School in Barrington, Rhode Island, was successful in getting businesses to contribute the literature as well as the blank tapes. The tapes, with the books and biographies of the different readers, were then sent to local children's hospitals in the surrounding area as a service-learning project (Cecil & Gipe, 2003).

For classes seeking more formal productions, stories can be adapted into more traditional plays portraying the physical actions of the characters, as shown in the activity below.

activity

Adapting Stories to Readers Theatre

The following steps, adapted from Cecil and Gipe (2003), briefly outline a spontaneous process for creating an adaptation of readers theatre that allows children's own words to "bring literature to life."

PROCEDURE

1. After setting a purpose for listening, read the story aloud for comprehension. Then have children read the story aloud with all the dramatic intensity they can muster.

2. Have several children relate the story in sequence from memory with the aid of a story grammar or story frame.

3. Select a scribe to write down the story, section by section, in the children's own words. Distribute copies of this new version to each child, thus providing each with a "script." (In a traditional play, the script is memorized; in readers theatre, it is simply read multiple times, thus increasing fluency.)

4. Have small groups of children act out, or "block," each section of the play as other children take turns reading it.

5. As a group, discuss how different characters might talk, walk, look, and behave. The roles of all characters should be considered in this discussion—from narrator to those involved in crowd scenes.

6. While the play is in rehearsal stage, tell the music teacher the theme of the upcoming performance and ask him or her to select several

songs that might enhance the script. Write the lyrics on an overhead transparency so that children can read and reread them until the songs are memorized.

CREATING ORIGINAL DRAMA

Perhaps the most exciting and language-enriching dramatic activities in the elementary classroom are the productions that children write and develop themselves for puppet shows, skits, and formal productions. When children move from acting out the ideas of others, as in using commercial scripts or readers theatre productions, to bringing their own *original* ideas to life, they experience the heady pride associated with owning a project from start to finish.

Children can study existing play scripts to learn the layout and specific conventions used in preparing scripts, as discussed in the previous sections. After children have read several plays in readers theatre format and have looked at commercial scripts, and after mini-lessons have reinforced the conventions used in script writing, the children can write an original script using their own creativity. Children will have become sufficiently adept at using commercial scripts when they can memorize or paraphrase their lines, speak them on cue, and create appropriate characterizations. As children go from reading and acting out the words of others to bringing their own words to life, they experience pride and a sense of ownership from the collaborative undertaking. Moreover, they increase their reading fluency due to multiple readings of the script that they and their classmates have authored.

Because creating scripts is one of the most ambitious tasks that can be undertaken in the field of drama, teachers should take steps to ensure a satisfying transition from having children adapt the works of others to trying their hands at actual play writing. Considering the following suggestions may be helpful (Cecil, 1994):

- Start small. Encourage children to begin with one-act skits.
- Divide children into small share groups, which will allow more equitable creative interchange for all group members.
- Provide several motivational prompts, or possible plot ideas, for each group to consider. Exhibit 4.2 identifies a structure that children can follow to create their own scripts.
- Do *not* use prompters for performances. Children will read and learn each other's lines when no adult is backstage providing cues.
- Although multiple readings of the script are desired to increase fluency, also encourage "spontaneous paraphrasing" of the script.

exhibit 4.2 Structure for creating original dramatic productions.

To help children create an original script, ask them to consider the following four essential elements that constitute a traditional drama:

1. ROLES (or identity)	2. PLACE (or situation)	3. FOCUS (or issue)	4. CONFLICT (or problem)
Who are you?	Where are you?	What is happening?	What problem needs to be solved?
Examples:	*Examples:*	*Examples:*	*Examples:*
A lost rabbit	the forest	finding courage	finding one's way
A spoiled child	a neighborhood	child makes others miserable	learning to share
A kind alien	a corn field	accepting differences	alien is feared

Source: Adapted from Block (2000).

After the teacher has helped each group brainstorm about the prompt they have chosen, or another that they have created themselves, a recorder in each group can write down the ideas on paper. The teacher can help by reminding children of the conventions of play writing that they have been exposed to through commercial plays as well as through readers theatre. The recorder can then enter the finished script into a word-processing program, with the help of the teacher if needed. Copies can be laminated and distributed to each child in the group. The repeated readings that are necessary for memorization of these original scripts will, again, provide an authentic purpose for multiple readings that lead to increased fluency.

Casting the actors for the original drama is often easier than for readers theatre plays because children generally create the same number of characters as there are in the group and usually "become" the character they were most instrumental in creating. In the rare case when casting the characters is problematic, however, children may "try out" for specific parts by reading their role with the appropriate dramatic intensity. The teacher can guide children to select the most appropriate choices by asking, "Which actor do you think was the most believable as the wolf? Why do you think so?" In this way, popularity-contest casting is largely avoided.

SUMMARY

Drama can be an extremely effective mode of self-expression through which children can develop fluency by way of motivated readings and rereadings of commercial, adapted, and children-authored scripts. Furthermore, children for whom English is a second language can become familiar with the special rhythm and cadence of the English language while they are beginning to grasp concepts and words that the actions in the drama portray.

Reading readily available commercial scripts allows children to become familiar with the particular style and conventions of the play as a discrete form of writing. With modeling from the teacher and proficient readers within the classroom, children can gain much practice reading with appropriate rate, expression, and ease.

Readers theatre is a form of drama that allows children to select favorite pieces of children's literature and make them into scripts that can be used for informal productions to be read in front of an audience. Through the use of one or more narrators to explain the scene and the action, their favorite stories can come to life and become authentic avenues for multiple readings that also serve to enhance fluency.

Finally, penning their own original plays for a more formal production offers children a viable outlet for creativity, while motivating them to read and reread as many times as necessary to memorize their own scripts.

The collaboration needed for each of these dramatic activities fosters a positive classroom climate and also provides the oral reading practice that children desperately need to become confident, fluent readers.

REFERENCES

Allington, R. L. (2001). *What really matters for struggling readers: Designing research-based programs.* New York: Addison-Wesley/Longman.

Block, C. C. (2000). *Teaching the language arts: Expanding thinking through student-centered instruction.* Needham Heights, MA: Allyn & Bacon.

Cecil, N. L., & Gipe, J. P. (2003). "Word study and fluency." In *Literacy in the intermediate grades: Best practices for a comprehensive program.* Scottsdale, AZ: Holcomb Hathaway.

Cecil, N. L., & Lauritzen, P. (1994). "Drama: Bringing ideas to life." In *Literacy and the arts in the integrated classroom.* New York: Longman.

Corathers, D. (Nov. 1991). Theatre education: Seeking balance between stage and classroom. *ASCD Curriculum Update, 12,* 12–17.

Edmiston, B., Encisco, P., & King, M. L. (1987). Empowering readers and writers through drama: Narrative theater. *Language Arts, 64,* 219–229.

Haven, K. F. (1996). *Great moments in science: Experiments and readers theatre*. Englewood, CO: Teach Idea Press.

Kane, S. (2007). *Literacy and learning in the content areas,* 2nd ed. Scottsdale, AZ: Holcomb Hathaway.

Martinez, M., Roser, N., & Strecker, S. (1999). "I never thought I could be a star": A readers' theatre ticket to fluency. *The Reading Teacher, 52,* 326–334.

Millin, S., & Rinehart, S. D. (1999). Some of the benefits of readers' theatre participation for second-grade title I students. *Reading Research and Instruction, 39,* 71–88.

Murphy, D. (2000). *Revolutionary War read-aloud plays*. New York: Scholastic.

Pugliano, C. (1998). *Easy-to-read folk and fairy tale plays*. New York: Scholastic.

Pugliano-Martin, C. (1999). *25 emergent reader plays around the year*. New York: Scholastic.

Pugliano-Martin, C. (2000). *Tall tales read-aloud plays*. New York: Scholastic.

Rasinski, T. V. (1999). Exploring a method for estimating independent, instructional, and frustration reading rates. *Reading Psychology: An International Quarterly, 20,* 61–69.

Rinehart, S. D. (1999). "Don't think for a minute that I'm getting up there": Opportunities for readers' theatre in a tutorial for children with reading problems. *Journal of Reading Psychology, 20,* 71–89.

Tompkins, G. E. (1998). *50 literacy strategies step by step*. Upper Saddle River, NJ: Merrill.

Tyler, B. J., & Chard, D. J. (2000). Using reader's theatre to foster fluency in struggling readers: A twist on the repeated readings strategy. *Reading & Writing Quarterly, 16,* 163–168.

Worthy, J., & Broaddus, K. (2001/2002). Fluency beyond the primary grades. From group performance to silent, independent reading. *The Reading Teacher, 55,* 334–343.

Yopp, R. H., & Yopp, H. K. (2003). Time with text. *The Reading Teacher, 57,* 284–287.

Young, T. A., & Vardell, S. (1993). Weaving readers theatre and nonfiction into the curriculum. *The Reading Teacher, 46,* 396–406.

Assisted Reading and Fluency

5

Previous chapters have addressed motivational ways to develop fluent readers through a host of best practices: literacy activities that are easily compatible with existing curricula and are supported by an abundance of research that provides evidence of their effectiveness. However, these instructional activities—drama, choral reading, community singing, and preparing pieces of literature for oral presentations—require a modicum of student independence or are conducted in large-group settings. In most cases, the teacher facilitates but provides little direct one-on-one instruction. For some children, however, whole-group lessons providing implicit instruction in fluency development will not suffice. These children are less independent in their ability to read fluently and need direct instruction in the underlying skills needed to help them become fluent readers. Offering feedback and guidance on their oral reading improves the effectiveness of fluency lessons for such learners, especially when the children read familiar text (National Institute of Child Health and Human Development, 2000).

This chapter contains a wide range of techniques for direct instruction in fluency development. Such techniques often are referred to as "assisted reading" and are generally used to promote fluency in readers. The chapter contains two sections of reading and fluency techniques, one for mainly teacher-directed activities, and the other for partner reading activities that can be accomplished with two carefully chosen students reading aloud to each other and providing each other with feedback about their reading fluency. Each section also contains guidelines for offering such feedback.

TEACHER-DIRECTED ASSISTED READING TECHNIQUES

The instructional techniques described in this section are typically used in one-to-one tutoring by the teacher, or with abundant teacher guidance; however, they may be adapted by pairing a child needing fluency help with a teacher's aide or a wisely chosen, fluent peer who can provide feedback and model the fluent reading of a proficient reader, thus assuming the role of teacher.

The Neurological Impress Method

The Neurological Impress Method (NIM) is much less intimidating than its rather formal name implies. Its name simply implies that the method helps the reader (the teacher) to affix the words in the child's brain. Using this method, the child and the teacher read orally in unison (Heckelman, 1969), with the teacher positioned slightly behind the child on the right side in order to read into the child's right ear. (Or one could read into the child's left ear, if the child prefers.) With a disfluent child, for whom this strategy is recommended (Richek, Caldwell, Jennings, & Lerner, 2002), the teacher's voice will actually be a bit ahead of the child's, especially if the child has a limited sight vocabulary. The two begin reading a passage on the child's instructional reading level, with the teacher modeling fluent, expressive reading and allowing the child, who is imitating the teacher, to experience how fluent reading feels. Because this method does take some getting used to, it is suggested that, initially, short, rhythmic, and repetitive passages, such as poems or song lyrics, might be helpful. (For suggestions, see Appendix A.)

Using NIM, the teacher does not stop and give feedback when the child struggles; instead, the child is instructed to continue to read along with the teacher as much as possible. The teacher may move an index card under the line of print being read so the child is able to track more easily. With increases in the child's fluency, the teacher's voice becomes softer, thereby reducing the modeling and allowing the child's reading to become dominant. Eventually, the child's voice leads the teacher's voice as more fluent reading begins to occur.

Bedsworth (1991) reported impressive gains for three children who used NIM only 10 minutes a day for nine weeks. All of the children made significant gains—3.5 years of improvement in tests of silent reading in fewer than four months of instruction. Moreover, the children's attitudes and self-perceptions about their reading became more positive. The reason for the gains, Bedsworth believes, is that NIM affords the learner the opportunity to follow along with an expert reader in a nonthreatening way. Also, the technique focuses the child's attention on the visual and auditory modalities, and the child is actually "trying on" the skill of reading in units rather than perpetuating the word-by-word reading customary in a disfluent reader. Although the original authors of this technique did not mention how comprehension improved using this method, I suggest following the procedure with open-ended questions ("Why do you think the boy never questioned his father about where he had gone?"), or reciprocal questioning ("I'll ask a question about the passage and then *you* ask *me* a question about the passage") to ensure that children understand that the focus on meaning is always paramount in reading.

Echo Reading

Echo reading was created to be a small-group strategy, although it can easily be used with individual children. Echo reading is similar to both NIM and repeated readings in that the child is following a teacher's model and may need to repeat, several times, the reading that is being imitated (Walker, 2000). In this method, though, the teacher reads one sentence of text aloud with appropriate phrasing and expression. The child then attempts to imitate this fluent oral-reading model. The text reading continues in this manner until the teacher feels the child is able to imitate more than one sentence at a time.

Echo reading allows children to read text more fluently than they would otherwise have been able to because of the initial modeling that occurs. The technique can be used together with repeated readings or NIM to model particularly troublesome sentences. Echo reading is particularly helpful for children who have a specific fluency skill deficit; for example, a child who reads in a monotone or a child who does not seem to understand that words carry meaning will benefit from hearing fluent reading, as the child is actually *shown* how to read fluently, one sentence at a time.

Use of Phrase Markings

Phrase marking (Fox, 2003) improves children's expression by helping them read in meaningful word groups. This is accomplished by having the teacher physically mark the phrase boundaries in text, through the use of colored highlighters or slashes, or by rewriting sentences using spaces between the phrases (see Exhibit 5.1). The child reads the text while adhering to the word groupings the teacher has identified.

exhibit 5.1 A phrase-marked passage.

The wounded cowboy/ could not move. /He struggled for a while/ and then lost consciousness./ Rambo, his dog,/ licked the cowboy's face/ with his tongue./ He tried to get/ the unconscious man/ to answer him/ but the cowboy/ did not stir./ Rambo finally ran/ to the road/ and howled./ Every once in a while/ he would trot back/ to the wounded man/ and try to wake him.

Using Phrase Markings to Increase Fluency

activity

The child can be encouraged to mark the word boundaries in a new passage, thinking aloud through the appropriate phrasing with the assistance of the teacher. Specifically, the following steps can be followed to use phrase markings to increase fluency.

PROCEDURE

1. Preview the passage to be read. Discuss the title, make connections with the child's background, and have the child make predictions about the passage.
2. Read the first sentence to the child. Make slashes where the ends of groupings would be and then read the sentence again, showing the

child how the slashes indicate where you pause in the reading. Do several more sentences in this fashion.

3. Ask the child to read the next sentence silently. Then invite the child to make slashes where the word group should end. The child then reads the sentence aloud, according to how the phrase has been marked.

4. Discuss where the child placed the slashes and if the sentence was indeed broken into meaningful units.

5. The teacher and child then take turns reading a sentence and marking the phrases using slashes or highlighting them using colored markers. The child may reread the passage several times to practice good phrasing.

6. Finally, the child is asked, "What was that passage about?" and is prompted to summarize the passage, including components of narrative structure if fictional text is used, or relevant facts and details if nonfiction material is used.

Skimming and Scanning

For most readers, fluency develops over time and through extensive reading. But fluency is *not* static, as novice readers mistakenly believe. A reader's level of fluency quite naturally varies, depending on the reader's familiarity with the words in the text, the subject matter of the material, and the purposes for reading. For example, one might read a mystery novel at a rapid pace, but studying a social studies chapter to prepare for a quiz would require much slower, more deliberate reading. Even very proficient adult readers may tend to read in a slow, laborious manner when confronted with material that contains highly technical vocabulary, or if the text addresses subjects of which they have little background knowledge. Children need direct instruction in knowing when to adjust their rate according to the text and their purposes for reading.

Two different kinds of in-class silent reading require a variation in normal fluency, as they are often done for purposes other than simple pleasure reading: skimming and scanning. Skimming is reading that is done rapidly, but purposefully, to get a general idea what a reading selection is about. Readers engaged in skimming will be expected to get the main idea of the selection as well as a few supporting details. Scanning, on the other hand, is pursued when a reader is looking for some specific information, such as when one is looking at the blurb on the back of a book to decide if one wishes to read it.

Both skimming and scanning are critical skills to teach for increasing fluency because they show children that reading rate is not a constant but changes for the purposes for which one is reading. In addition, both skimming and scanning are discrete reading skills that encourage children to push themselves to read at a faster than normal rate while still attending to comprehension.

Practice in Skimming

An effective way to practice skimming with children is to incorporate it as a regular routine when introducing new chapters in content-area material, such as science or social studies, using the following procedure:

- Before beginning the chapter, ask children to look through or "skim" the chapter to get a general idea of what it might contain. Tell them to pay particular attention to boldfaced headings, section titles, the introduction, and the summary.
- Invite them to jot down their ideas about the possible content of the chapter and share those ideas with the rest of the class.
- When the children have completed the chapter, ask them to revisit their ideas to see if they were correct.
- This activity can eventually be timed to reinforce for children that skimming should be done more rapidly than normal reading.

A variation on this activity would be to have students skim sports articles to determine why their favorite sports team won or lost.

Practice in Scanning

Scanning abilities can be fostered by encouraging children to locate specific information from reference material, such as *TV Guide,* the telephone book, an encyclopedia, or an almanac. For example, using the telephone directory, children can be asked to find the telephone number of a particular person or the number of the nearest pizza restaurant. Similarly, children can scan news articles to find out the what, why, where, and when of a recent event. To enhance student interest and increase speed, make the activity into a teamed competition, pairing an empathic but rapid reader with one who may need more assistance.

Fluency-Oriented Reading Instruction

One group activity for assisted reading combines teacher-assisted reading with partner reading. This promising intervention program, *fluency-oriented reading instruction (FORI),* connects the research-based practices of repeated readings with independent, silent reading within a three-part classroom program, set up and partially assisted by the teacher.

The three components of FORI are

- a reading lesson that includes teacher-led, repeated oral reading and partner reading
- a free reading period at school
- prescribed at-home reading

This fluency intervention program produced gains of almost two years in second-grade students (Stahl, 2002; Stahl, Heubach, & Cramond, 1996).

Using Fluency-Oriented Reading Instruction

The following are the steps in FORI.

PROCEDURE

1. The teacher initiates the activity by modeling the reading of a story or passage, modeling correct expression, phrasing, and attention to punctuation. Although the passage can be fiction or nonfiction, it should be highly motivational and on the children's independent reading level.

2. After the reading, the teacher solicits the children's responses to the selection, gauging appreciation for the story and making sure children understand what has been read.

3. The teacher then reviews key vocabulary and concepts and has children engage in comprehension activities built around the reading. For example, the children might make a recording of themselves orally retelling the sequence of events in an expository piece about penguins in small share groups, or they might act out scenes from a story about a wounded knight, one group at a time.

4. The children then take the selection home and, with prior instructions to parents or other caregivers (e.g., "Simply listen to your child read this passage and provide positive feedback."), read it aloud an additional time.

5. The following day, children reread the selection in pairs. One child reads a page as the other child monitors the reading. Then the partners switch roles for another page. This continues until the text is finished.

6. After the partner reading, the teacher leads extension activities that can cross the curriculum, such as having the children research the continent of Antarctica after reading an expository piece on penguins.

activity

7. In the independent reading phase of FORI, time is reserved later in the day for children to select their own reading material, at their independent reading level, to practice the skills leading to reading fluency in a nonstructured way. Optionally, they may do oral reading with partners during this time.

Oral Recitation Lesson

The *oral recitation lesson (ORL)* is another fluency instruction intervention that contains the key ingredients of effective fluency instruction and provides teacher assistance and modeling (Hoffman, 1987; Hoffman & Crone, 1985). Like the other teacher-assisted techniques described earlier, it too has been reported to lead to increased gains in fluency, but it also has a major focus on comprehension and appears to improve scores in that component of literacy as well (Reutzel & Hollingsworth, 1993).

The ORL can be used in both whole-group and small-group situations, and contains both direct and indirect instruction.

activity

Initiating an Oral Recitation Lesson

The following steps are recommended in initiating an ORL.

PROCEDURE

1. The teacher reads a story to children and then guides them in discussing and analyzing it.
2. From the discussion, the teacher helps the children to create a story map or story grammar summarizing the key elements in the story.
3. Using the story map or story grammar, each child creates a written summary of the story.
4. The teacher selects certain segments of the story and models reading them aloud, calling attention to different features of fluent oral reading, such as effective oral expression.
5. The children imitate the teacher's reading, both individually and chorally.
6. Individual children "perform" the reading of self-selected parts of the story for small groups of children, while the impromptu audience offers praise and positive comments.

7. For ten minutes daily, the children practice reading portions of the story by themselves, using a kind of "whisper reading." The teacher listens to each child, checking progress using anecdotal notes.

Tape-Assisted Reading

One of the most frustrating concerns with teacher-assisted reading in the classroom is that it takes a considerable amount of time and that it often requires much one-on-one teacher support, or guidance and observation from the teacher, for each child. It is difficult, in a class of twenty-five students, for a teacher to find even five minutes a day to listen to and provide feedback for each child (Adams, 2002). Tape-assisted reading can help. As first described by Chomsky (1978), children read along in a book while listening to the text that has been recorded by a fluent reader. For the first reading, the child follows along in a copy of the reading selection, using a finger (with early readers) or an index card (with older or more advanced readers) to track the one-to-one correspondence of the spoken and printed words. After listening to the entire selection in this fashion, the child chooses one favorite part of the passage to read and practice. She finds the passage on the tape and rehearses the chosen passage along with the tape, repeatedly, until she can read it fluently and independently. Finally, when she feels comfortable with the reading, she "performs" the passage for the teacher.

The results of studies looking at tape-assisted reading have been largely positive. For example, Koskinen and colleagues (1999) found that using tape-assisted reading for children for whom English is a second language produced a significant increase in general reading achievement, interest, and self-confidence. Surprisingly, in a study by Biemiller and Shany (1995), third- and fourth-grade children who participated in tape-assisted readings actually scored higher than children who had participated in teacher-guided repeated readings in measures of both reading and comprehension.

STUDENT- AND PARENT-ASSISTED FLUENCY TECHNIQUES

Various forms of oral partner-reading activities have been found to produce significant improvements in fluency (Eldredge, 1990). Oral-reading experiences involving pairs of children have at least two advantages:

- A large number of children can gain fluency practice simultaneously.

- Both children in each pair are actively involved at all times, either as reader or listener.

One first-grade teacher who underscored the benefits of partner reading in her classroom observed that the children seemed to enjoy taking on the role of the teacher. She offers that, "I see children taking pride in helping their friends be successful as readers rather than making fun of the errors made" (Eldredge, 1990, p. 80).

Teachers can train the partners by modeling the process, using one set of partners to demonstrate how to read, listen, and ask good questions. Partners can be told to ask "why?" questions, or open-ended questions for which there is no one right answer. A proficient reader can also be taught how to offer feedback to a struggling reader about word-recognition strategies, as will be discussed later in this chapter. As soon as pairs of children are competent enough to carry out the alternate reading/listening/questioning process, they can be invited to read to each other independently. The teacher continues to meet with other pairs until all children are prepared to read and question without teacher direction.

In another version of partner reading, a proficient reader is paired with a struggling reader. The teacher first reads a text aloud (usually at the struggling reader's instructional reading level), pointing to words as they are read and modeling appropriate phrasing and expression, while the children follow along in their own books. Then the partners take turns reading a section of the text to each other, with the proficient reader beginning, imitating the teacher's fluency. Next the struggling reader reads aloud the same section of the text, as the partner provides word-recognition assistance, feedback, and praise. The struggling reader rereads the section of text until it can be read fluently without guidance (Samuels, 2002).

Dyad Reading

To focus on comprehension when reading orally, especially when reading expository text, children can be taught to use dyad reading (Cecil & Gipe, 2003). This strategy is yet another variation on partner reading, although the children need not be paired according to reading ability.

To demonstrate this strategy, the teacher can select two children to sit at the front of the class. The first child reads aloud a sentence or paragraph from the text (depending on the grade level) and the second child listens carefully and then orally summarizes the content of what the first child read. For variety, or with English language learners, the second child can simply draw the main ideas of what was read and then discuss the picture. The children then switch roles, with the reader becoming the summarizer. The reading continues this way until the passage is completed.

Parent Partners

After including parents in a plan to improve children's skills, teachers in two third-grade classes observed increased proficiency in oral fluency (Ross, 1986). After informing parents that teachers would be evaluating children's oral reading fluency every Friday, the teachers asked the parents to have their children read assigned pages from the selected literature every night for practice. A note was sent home to parents, telling them exactly which skills their child needed to practice; for example, one child might need to work on stopping for appropriate punctuation and another might need to phrase words in natural speech patterns. Standards for oral fluency were discussed in class, and children were shown the procedures to use at home, such as how to chart their comprehension progress using a simple bar graph showing both rate *and* comprehension (see Exhibit 5.2). Selections assigned to children were at their independent reading level to permit fluent oral reading free of word recognition errors.

TEACHERS AND PEERS AS FLUENCY COACHES

The assisted reading techniques mentioned above have all been shown to be effective in increasing fluency and, in many cases, reading comprehension as well. However, I believe that the quality of the feedback, or coaching, that is offered to a struggling reader by a more

exhibit 5.2 Bar graph showing reading rate and comprehension.

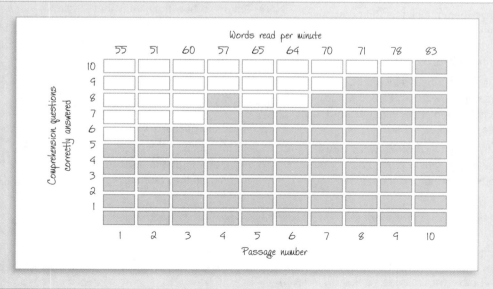

fluent one may be even more important than the instructional method that is used. The amount, sensitivity, and nature of the feedback given to children about their fluency performance, in part, determines how well the child responds to the reading sessions. See Exhibit 5.3 for techniques to provide feedback to a struggling reader about word recognition skills.

exhibit 5.3   Helping children tackle challenging words.

When a reader gets stuck on a word, always wait five seconds before intervening!

When readers lose their place or skip words:

- Have them point to each word.

When readers stop because they do not know the word:

- Have them read to the end of the sentence and ask them what would make sense.
- Have them look at the picture for clues.
- Have them read the sentence with what they think the word is and ask if that word makes sense.
- Have them check their first response with the spelling of the written word and ask them if that looks like the written word.
- If their response is incorrect, provide the correct word and ask them to read the sentence with that word to see if it makes sense.
- If there is a part of the word they know (*e.g., am* in *ham*), cover with your finger the part they do not know

and ask them to read the part they do. Then ask them to try again

When readers read incorrect words:

- Read the sentence to the student as they have just read it and ask them if it makes sense.
- Ask them if their response matches the printed word.
- Help them find familiar elements in the printed word.
- Have them reread the sentence with the new word and ask them if that makes sense.

When readers self-correct:

- Ask them how they knew that the first response was incorrect.
- Ask them how they figured out the correct word.
- Compliment them on using the strategy!

When readers do not pause for periods:

- Read the passage back to the students and ask them if it sounds correct.
- Have them point to periods in the same manner as they point to words.

Source: Adapted from Johnston, F., Invernizzi, M., & Juel, C. (1998). *Book buddies: Guidelines for volunteer tutors of emergent and early readers.* New York: The Guilford Press; and DeVries, B. A. (2004). *Literacy assessment and intervention for the elementary classroom.* Scottsdale, AZ: Holcomb Hathaway.

The Teacher

Three pedagogical factors contribute to teachers' effectiveness as coaches in literacy in general and in fluency in particular (Clark, 2004). The first factor is an understanding of phonics and English spellings. Teachers need to know how words are put together and the rules that govern the grapheme-phoneme in order to explain those rules to their students as necessary. Second, they must take anecdotal records as they assist the learner in order to keep track of each child's instructional history. Finally, they must be aware of each child's specific strengths and limitations in order, during each tutoring situation, to help the child apply the skills that she already possesses and to move her developmentally toward the skills she lacks.

Other issues concern how to offer feedback. For example, when a child is reading orally for the teacher and makes a mistake, especially one that changes the meaning of the text, such as misreading or mispronouncing a word, the teacher should pause for a moment to see whether or not the child will correct the error independently. If the child does not do so, the teacher should gently direct the child's attention to clues about the word's pronunciation or meaning. When the word is correctly identified and read, the teacher should immediately nod, offer praise, or otherwise give the child a "thumbs up." Then the teacher should ask the child to reread the sentence that contained the word to help the child assimilate the correction and recover the meaning of the sentence.

Finally, in tutoring sessions, teachers need to remember that every child is different. When listening to children read, the teacher must gauge their level of frustration to decide exactly how long to continue and how much feedback to offer them in any one session. Signs of frustration include sighing, squirming, eye-rubbing, distractibility, and complaining. When children are manifesting such symptoms, the session should be quickly terminated.

Student Tutors

One of the biggest considerations in student partner reading is often choosing the pairs. Generally, the teacher pairs a struggling reader with an empathic, proficient reader, hoping that the struggling reader will reap many of the same benefits as would occur if the teacher were working with the child. Some research has suggested that children who pick their own pairs tend to work better together, however, as there are fewer arguments and, thus, more time spent on task (Meisinger, Schwanenflugel, Bradley, Kuhn, & Stahl, 2002). On the other hand, Labbo and Teale (1990) suggest pairing two struggling readers—an older child and a younger child. Such pairing has been shown to produce fluency gains for both readers.

No matter how the children are paired for assisted reading, instruction should always be focused on two major results: (1) both children should have the opportunity to increase fluency through oral reading practice, and (2) struggling readers should see a model of how a more fluent reader reads and obtain feedback about their fluency and how to improve it.

Children should be trained by the teacher to offer corrective feedback to one another. The teacher should first model partner reading with a proficient reader in front of the class, telling the child exactly what errors to pretend to make, so the teacher can demonstrate how to give appropriate feedback, as in the following example (Osborn & Lehr, 2003):

CHILD: *(reading)* "I would like to choose that toy to give to my *bother* for his birthday," exclaimed the boy.

TEACHER: *(pointing to the italicized word)* Stop. Let's look again. This word is *brother,* not *bother.* Can you see the difference between these two words in how they look and how they sound? Brother has a /br/. Brother, bother. Hear the difference? Now you say the word.

CHILD: Brother.

TEACHER: Great! Now read the whole sentence again.

CHILD: "I would like to choose that toy to give to my brother for his birthday," exclaimed the boy.

SUMMARY

In order to become fluent readers, children often need direct instruction, with subsequent practice, in how to acquire such important skills. Teachers can sometimes assist, providing direct instruction. They can show children how to use word recognition strategies, how to phrase appropriately, and how to read with expression to make the story come to life. Likewise, other children can be taught how to offer feedback to struggling readers, as both children find themselves in a motivational, social setting for reading and responding to text. Such attention to oral reading in the classroom will go a long way toward fostering reading fluency. Yet fluency is only one aspect of literacy. The teacher must always keep in mind that understanding what is read is always at the heart of any effective literacy program.

REFERENCES

Adams, M. J. (2002, November 7). The promise of speech recognition. PowerPoint presentation presented at A Focus on Literacy Forum, San Francisco, CA. Available at: www.prel.org/programs/rel/fluency/Adams.ppt.

Bedsworth, B. (1991). The neurological impress method with middle school poor readers. *Journal of Reading, 34,* 534–565.

Biemiller, A., & Shany, M. T. (1995). Assisted reading practice: Effects on performance for poor readers in grades 3 and 4. *Reading Research Quarterly, 30,* 382–395.

Cecil, N. L., & Gipe, J. P. (2003). *Literacy in the intermediate grades: Best practices for a comprehensive program.* Scottsdale, AZ: Holcomb Hathaway.

Chomsky, C. (1978). When you still can't read in third grade after decoding, what? In S. J. Samuels (Ed.), *What research has to say about reading instruction* (pp. 13–30). Newark, DE: International Reading Association.

Clark, K. F. (2004). What can I say besides "sound it out"? Coaching word recognition in beginning reading. *The Reading Teacher, 57,* 440–449.

DeVries, B. A. (2004). Literacy assessment and intervention for the elementary classroom. Scottsdale, AZ: Holcomb Hathaway.

Eldredge, J. L. (1990). Increasing the performance of poor readers in the third grade with a group-assisted strategy. *Journal of Educational Research, 84,* 69–77.

Fox, B. J. (2003). *Word recognition activities: Patterns and strategies for developing fluency.* Upper Saddle River, NJ: Merrill/Prentice Hall.

Giard, M. (1993). Bringing children to literacy through guided reading. In B. Harp (Ed.), *Bringing children to literacy: Classrooms at work.* Norwood, MA: Christopher-Gordon.

Heckelman, R. G. (1969). A neurological impress method of remedial reading instruction. *Academic Therapy, 4,* 277–282.

Hoffman, J. V. (1987). Rethinking the role of oral reading in basal instruction. *Elementary School Journal, 87,* 367–373.

Hoffman, J. V., & Crone, S. (1985). The oral recitation lesson: A research-derived strategy for reading basal texts. In J. A. Niles & R. A. Lalik (Eds.), *Issues in literacy: A research perspective. Thirty-fourth yearbook of the National Reading Conference* (pp. 76–83). Rochester, NY: National Reading Conference.

Johnston, F., Invernizzi, M., & Juel, C. (1998). *Book buddies: Guidelines for volunteer tutors of emergent and early readers.* New York: The Guilford Press.

Koskinen, P. S., Blum, I. H., Bisson, S. A., Phillips, S. M., Creamer, T. S., & Baker, T. K. (1999). Shared reading, books, and audiotapes: Supporting diverse students in school and at home. *The Reading Teacher, 52,* 430–444.

Labbo, L. D., & Teale, W. H. (1990). Cross age tutoring: A strategy for helping poor readers. *The Reading Teacher, 43,* 363–369.

Meisinger, E. B., Schwanenflugel, P. J., Bradley, E., Kuhn, M. R., & Stahl, S. A. (2002, December). *Interaction quality during partner reading.* Paper presented at the annual meeting of the National Reading Conference, Miami, FL.

National Institute of Child Health and Human Development. (2000). *Report of the Reading Panel: Teaching children to read: An evidence-based assessment of the scientific research literature on reading and its implications for reading instruction.* Reports of the subgroups. (NIH Publication No. 00-4754). Washington, D.C.: U.S. Government Printing Office.

Osborn, J. O., & Lehr, F. L. (2003). *A focus on fluency.* Honolulu, HI: Pacific Resources for Education and Learning.

Reutzel, D. R., & Hollingsworth, P. M. (1993). Effects of fluency training on second graders' reading comprehension. *Journal of Educational Research, 86,* 325–331.

Richek, M. A., Caldwell, J. S., Jennings, J. H., & Lerner, J. W. (2002). *Reading problems: Assessment and teaching strategies,* 4th ed. Boston: Allyn & Bacon.

Ross, E. P. (1986). Classroom experiments with oral language. *The Reading Teacher, 40,* 270–275.

Samuels, S. J. (2002). Reading fluency: Its development and assessment. In E. Farstrup & S. J. Samuels (Eds.), *What research has to say about reading instruction* (3rd ed., pp. 166–183). Newark, DE: International Reading Association.

Stahl, S. A. (2002, November 7). Fluency: Instruction and assessment. PowerPoint presentation presented at A Focus on Fluency Forum, San Francisco, CA. Available at: www.prel.org/programs/rel/fluency/Stahl.ppt.

Stahl, S. A., Heubach, K., & Cramond, B. (1996). *Fluency oriented reading instruction* (NRRC Report No. 79). College Park, MD: National Reading Research Center.

Walker, B. J. (2000). *Diagnostic teaching of reading: Techniques for instruction and assessment,* 4th ed. Upper Saddle River, NJ: Merrill/Prentice Hall.

Independent Silent Reading and Fluency Development 6

Most programs designed to increase fluency tend to focus on oral reading, although the value of activities created to improve silent reading must also be considered, especially as children move into the intermediate grades. While much early instruction and diagnosis are accomplished through having children read orally, the reality of most subsequent reading experience is that it tends to occur independently and silently. Therefore, activities that are designed to help children read silently—and motivate them to wish to do so as a chosen recreational activity—are an important facet of any book purporting to foster reading fluency.

Appropriately, Keith Stanovich (1986) calls the phenomenon the "Matthew Effect": Just as the Bible proclaims that "the rich get richer and the poor get poorer," those children who read frequently, through the constant practice this affords, become richer—although in an academic rather than financial sense. Through repeated practice decoding words and memorizing sight vocabulary, they become more fluent readers, both silently *and* orally. And because they become more fluent and feel successful, they tend to read even *more*. A chain of events is set into motion that clearly favors the children who read the most. On the other hand, those hapless children who struggle to decode and thus fail to acquire fluency tend to avoid reading, and thus they do not get the ample practice needed to improve the skills necessary for literacy. For these struggling readers, fluency is elusive. This delay in fluency, in theory, inhibits comprehension and vocabulary growth (Cunningham and Stanovich, 1998). Not surprisingly, a good deal of correlational research shows a possible predictive relationship between amount of reading practice occurring and the resultant reading success. For example, Juel (1988) found that first graders who read more had better word recognition skills than those children who read less. Similarly, Taylor, Pearson, Clark, and Walpole (1999) found evidence to support a conclusion that those classes where children had high reading achievement were classes in which silent independent reading occurred on a regular basis. Finally, Krashen (1994) synthesized research in fluency that strongly suggests that self-selected, voluntary reading, outside of direct instructional time, is a viable formula for developing fluent readers. Getting children motivated to read because they choose to do so—when so many attractive pursuits are vying for their limited free time—necessitates that teachers spend time fostering positive attitudes toward reading.

Besides creating a positive attitude toward reading, the challenge for today's teachers is to find many varied opportunities for meaningful silent-reading practice so that children can practice the skills of reading, thus becoming fluent. Historically, there have been two ways to give children the reading practice they need to become fluent readers. The first is to allot a special time during the school day for children to experience the reading of self-selected texts in order to build enjoyment and to provide reading practice. This practice is supported by Fielding and Pearson (1994), who suggest that, as a rule of thumb, the amount of time spent *actually reading* in class should equal or exceed the total amount of time learning the skills of reading.

The second way to provide silent reading practice is for teachers to use motivational techniques and classroom incentives that encourage children to read recreationally, at home, thus conserving valuable classroom time for direct instruction.

This chapter is divided into two sections, based on these two important ways to provide silent reading practice for children.

FOSTERING INDEPENDENT READING IN CLASS

W hile the majority of reading practice that children undertake should ideally be accomplished at home, teachers must accomplish two tasks while the children are in the classroom. The first is to instill in learners a love for reading so they will willingly choose to read when they are home and when many attractions are competing for their free time. The second is to provide specific instructional activities that allow children to practice reading in ways that cause them to become more accurate, fluent readers who can adjust their reading rate according to the purposes for which they are reading.

Developing a Classroom Climate That Fosters Autonomy

It seems axiomatic that developing positive attitudes toward reading starts with a positive classroom climate, where children have a modicum of choice and control over what they read and choose to learn. Oldfather (2001) suggests that a "responsive classroom culture" is the best environment in which to motivate children to read and to learn. Such a culture develops a community of learners that promotes low anxiety, risk taking, and caring, and includes the following features:

- Teachers explain the purpose of reading and writing assignments.
- Learning is considered more important than getting the correct answer.
- Each child is expected to contribute and is responded to.
- Making mistakes is considered an integral part of the learning process.
- Students choose books but also read core curriculum texts.
- Students' interests and suggestions help form the curriculum.
- The cultural, linguistic, and ethnic diversity of the class and the community is reflected in the books contained in the classroom library.

Concept-Oriented Reading Instruction

Another approach to developing independent reading is through a curriculum plan called *concept-oriented reading instruction (CORI)* (Guthrie & McCann, 1997). The creators of this plan used it with third- and fifth-grade classrooms as an instructional context to develop motivation in expository reading and learning in the content areas. In this context, one containing many similarities to the responsive classroom culture, children are encouraged to do the following:

- Initiate their own reading and research topics
- Direct their own work
- Collaborate with classmates
- Assess their own learning
- Show their new understandings in creative and personally meaningful ways

Using such a program, the teacher facilitates and answers questions but lets the children determine how they will spend their CORI time, which usually consists of a block of time such as one hour three or four times a week. After three years of piloting the CORI plan, Guthrie and McCann (1997) found that the self-determination afforded by the plan resulted in children with high intrinsic motivation. These children devised their own effective strategies to find books and other resources, and were highly capable of reading and researching without becoming distracted, as compared with children in more traditional programs. For more information about CORI, visit www.cori.umd.edu.

In-Class Silent Reading

Another essential component of fostering independent reading, according to Guthrie and McCann (1997), appears to be assigning some portions of the class day to a special time when children are able to control their own destinies and select for themselves the material they would like to read. For years, teachers have been operationalizing this concept by setting aside a brief period of time when children could do "free reading" of their own choice, offering the rationale that this unstructured time would give children time to practice the skills of fluency and comprehension that had been taught in the more teacher-directed portions of the school day. Moreover, attitudes toward reading have been shown to become more positive when free-reading time is set aside. Weisendanger and Birlem (1984) found that 9 of the 11 studies they analyzed presented evidence that students develop more positive attitudes toward reading, and tend to read more, when a free-reading time is instituted in classes. In her study, Valeri-Gold (1995) supported these findings, as she reported that the majority of students in her class admitted to reading more in their own free time as a result of reading started in her class, and they held more favorable attitudes toward reading.

After thoroughly examining a wealth of research articles, the National Reading Panel (2000) neither endorsed nor rejected the idea of instituting a specified silent reading time in the classroom as a way to build reading fluency. Although some studies they reviewed showed a positive correlation with increased achievement in reading, the Panel pointed out that a correlation does not imply that the reading improvement was *caused* by the recreational in-school reading. The Panel's additional concern was that such practices could conceivably take valuable direct skill instruction time away from the children most in need of it. A further concern was that when students read silently, it is difficult to evaluate their fluency and provide appropriate feedback to correct underlying problems with it (Shanahan, 2002); moreover, because children are not usually held accountable for what they read in these unstructured sessions, some children often engage in off-task behaviors during this time, such as day-dreaming, walking around the room, and distracting other children, instead of actually reading. These concerns can be addressed by conducting the silent reading sessions in a way that makes them more productive for fluency development. To revise the practice of in-class silent reading, Anderson (1990) suggests that teachers show children how to self-select appropriate reading material, provide time for children to respond to what they have read, and directly observe children while they read.

Guidelines for In-Class Silent Reading

Make instruction in how to self-select appropriate reading material an essential part of the silent reading program. As an example, teach children to select books on their independent reading level. One method of doing this is called the *rule of thumb method,* whereby children are taught to turn to a page at random from the middle of a book they wish to read. They then start reading the page and hold up one finger every time they come to a word they cannot pronounce or for which they do not know the meaning. If they get all the way to their thumb, the book is deemed too difficult and they may want to choose another book.

Another method for teaching children to choose books is the *Goldilocks method* (Ohlausen & Jepson, 1992). Using this approach, children browse through several books that appear to be interesting. Then, initially with the aid of the teacher but later by themselves, they place the books into three piles. One pile is for "too easy" books, the second "too hard" books, and the third "just right" books.

Using either of these methods encourages children to spend a small amount of time upfront helping to ensure that the books chosen will offer enough of a challenge to keep them engaged yet will not overly frustrate them. If, despite the use of these methods, a child consistently chooses material far above or below her independent reading level, a teacher may bend the "free choice" privilege. With information from the results of a reading interest inventory (see Appendix B), the teacher may then select several books that might appeal to the child and that are also at the child's appropriate independent reading level, from which the child may choose.

Provide time for children to respond to what they have read silently. Adults seem to enjoy book clubs because such structured social communications deepen their appreciation of a book by allowing them to crystallize their feelings about what they have read with others; children have a similar need for a social sharing of their reactions to what they have read. They can do so through *book clubs,* where everyone who has read the same book meets to discuss personal reactions, or through interest groups, where all children interested in reading about one topic, or books written by the same author, can share their literacy experiences.

They can also do *book talks,* where they think of innovative ways to recommend a book they are reading to others. Such an activity might include reading the blurb on the back of the book in the same way a radio announcer might while selling a product (see Chapter 2), or giving a testimonial, with the child sharing favorite excerpts along with his or her personal feelings about the book (see Exhibit 6.1). Finally, children can keep a literature response journal of sentences or paragraphs from the book that they find particularly funny, poignant, interesting, scary, and so forth, and share excerpts from their journals in small groups. Exhibit 6.2 provides an excerpt from the response journal of third-grade Nadya, who is reading *Deborah Sampson Goes to War* by Bryna Stevens (Dell, 1984).

exhibit 6.1 A book talk by Juli, grade 3.

I read the book *Kahu the Cautious Kiwi,* by Brian Birchall. If you like exciting books about different countries, and you like animals, you will love this book. Kahu is a kiwi, a kind of bird that lives in New Zealand. He gets chased by a dog, and then a wild cat. Then he gets his leg caught in a trap and it looks like he will be eaten by the wild cat. But then a kind boy saves his life. What will happen next? Will Kahu stay with the boy or go back to the bush, where he used to live? You won't believe the ending! I really recommend this book, especially for animal lovers!

exhibit 6.2 Sample literature response journal.

"If men can fight for freedom," she wondered, "why can't I?" (p. 12)

I asked my mom that question the other day. She said women DO go to war, but in the olden days they didn't used to.

Directly observe children as they are reading. Although teachers should spend the majority of this voluntary reading time modeling the reading act themselves, occasionally the teacher may also want to sit and watch children's behavior unobtrusively as they read. Such observations will confirm that children are actually reading, but they can also yield a tremendous amount of information to the astute observer about the individual reading habits and attitudes of each child in the class. A checklist can help to prompt and record observations about children (see Exhibit 6.3).

exhibit 6.3 Sample checklist for observing students during silent reading.

Silent Reading Checklist

Date: _____

	Benjamin	Chao	Hannah	Juanita
Which children appear so engrossed in reading that they are reluctant to put down their book?	○	○	○	○
Which students appear easily distracted or appear to day-dream?	○	○	○	○
Which students finger-point or subvocalize?	○	○	○	○
Which students rub their eyes or hold the book too closely as they read?	○	○	○	○
Which children need additional help selecting books on their independent reading level?	○	○	○	○
Which children appear to need additional help selecting books that match their interests?	○	○	○	○

Sustained Silent Reading Time

A specific program for self-selected reading time, sometimes known as *SSR* (*sustained silent reading*) or *DEAR* (*drop everything and read*), consists of a set time each day when children select material to read, simply to practice the reading skills that they have acquired in other times of the day. The goal is for children to develop reading fluency, deepen comprehension, and develop a love for reading that will extend far beyond the classroom doors. The rationale for this program suggests that, if children see the value in reading and continue to choose to read in their own free time, more reading practice is gained and a self-perpetuating march toward increased fluency has begun. Such reading practice time can serve many purposes, including the following:

- Because most school reading is assigned, SSR allows children an opportunity to read material of their own choosing.
- During free reading time, many children learn that they can use their word-attack skills to figure out new words on their own.
- Free reading time can help build children's confidence in their ability to work through trouble spots in reading.
- Many studies of whole-class groups and select groups of reluctant readers indicate that in-school free reading can result in children desiring to read more.
- Because of free reading time in school, the amount of time that children spend reading outside of school often increases, according to parents.
- A free reading time can be a crucial element in a reading program that demonstrates that reading is a joyful and worthwhile activity.
- Time spent reading is correlated with vocabulary growth, fluency in word recognition, and comprehension (Yopp & Yopp, 2003).

To initiate this practice of SSR, a teacher should administer a reading interest inventory (see Appendix B) to every child in the class to get an idea of what types of reading materials will engage each child. In the classroom library, the teacher should have abundant reading materials that match those interests, as well as a variety of other reading materials, such as these:

- Informational texts
- Books of all genres
- Children's magazines (*Cricket, Ranger Rick, National Geographic World, Sports Illustrated for Kids,* etc.)

- Books representing a variety of cultures and ethnicities (especially those that are found in the classroom and the community)
- Comic books
- Almanacs and other reference books
- Books in languages that reflect the home languages of the children in the class
- Catalogues and travel brochures

The teacher should then set aside a consistent time each day—usually 10 minutes for early primary grades and up to 30 for older children—when children can read, uninterrupted by any other events. Worthy and Broaddus (2002) suggest beginning with about 10 minutes each day and increasing to about 35 minutes each day as the children become capable of maintaining their attention and motivation for a longer time. To initiate the program, some teachers like to start with a very brief amount of time and then gradually extend it as they see more and more children becoming engrossed in reading and reluctantly putting their books away at the end of the session.

To ensure that there are no distractions, each child should gather books in advance, so that no valuable reading time is spent in searching for materials. No written assignments should be attempted at this time, nor is talking or asking questions allowed. The teacher, too, participates in the reading time, thus modeling reading behavior. The only sounds should be the occasional chuckle from a reader. Ideally, the entire school participates in the program, thus guaranteeing that no announcements, visitors, or maintenance issues will interrupt the reading sessions. With the whole school making this commitment, a clear statement is made that all who dwell in the school value reading as an important and worthwhile activity.

To ensure its effectiveness, the teacher and students should, collaboratively, set guidelines for silent reading time behavior. Among the most critical of these guidelines are that (1) everyone must be reading *something,* (2) there is no talking, and (3) there is no writing or doing homework at this time. Note: Teachers must be consistent and patient when establishing SSR as a new routine. Because it will seem unstructured compared with the rest of their instructional day, some children may try to use the time to be social or off-task. With firm reminders of the expected behaviors—and a modicum of patience—children will usually begin to look forward to this break in the structured routine.

After the silent reading session, a brief time should be set aside for children to share their ideas about what they have read through oral discussions, book clubs, or sharing excerpts from their response logs, as discussed earlier.

FOSTERING INDEPENDENT
SILENT READING AT HOME

T o develop optimal fluency and comprehension skills, children must continue to engage in literate activities beyond the classroom setting. As in school, silent reading is a natural way for children to enhance their fluency skills. But to motivate children to choose to read at home requires that teachers begin to focus on the affective aspects of literacy in the classroom that will transfer to the home, actively seeking to develop positive attitudes and interests in reading and writing, as well as finding a host of creative ways to point out the value of literacy in children's daily lives.

Incentives

A number of programs sponsored by large corporations seem to be successful at motivating children to read at home in order to receive appealing gifts and prizes. Although many educators believe that "reading should be its own reward," several studies demonstrate that the use of tangible incentives, such as prizes, under certain conditions can enhance intrinsic motivation, or the desire to read more. Studies have determined that if a valued reward is offered (1) when the level of interest is low, (2) when the attractiveness of the activity will become apparent after engaging in it over time, or 3) when a certain level of mastery needs to be attained, then the reward may lead to greater intrinsic motivation (Lepper, Greene, & Nisbett, 1973; McLoyd, 1979).

Therefore, it appears that programs such as the All American Reading Challenge (sponsored by McDonald's, the American Library Association, and Scholastic), Book It! (sponsored by Pizza Hut), Bucks for Books (sponsored by the Earning by Learning Foundation), and RUNNING START (sponsored by Reading Is Fundamental) can be effective for increasing intrinsic motivation. While verbal praise and positive feedback increase intrinsic motivation, due to their informational and affective value, personal choice is also a powerful incentive and is likely the reason that the sponsored reading programs—and any approaches that encourage self-selected reading—in the classroom are successful: Children enjoy being in control of what they will read. In fact, the research is most clear on the strong positive correlation between choice and the development of intrinsic motivation (Turner, 1995).

Similar incentives can be used in schools by holding reading challenges, whereby a class is challenged to read a certain number of books in order to win a party, field trip, or special event. One school in Kentucky had an overnight Read In, where children brought their sleeping bags and camped out in the library. They were allowed to stay up as late as they liked—as long as they were reading. One school principal in Sacramento, California, told the children in the school that she would dye her hair green if they could read a specified number of books by the end of the year. The children met the challenge—and the plucky principal kept her end of the bargain by acquiring a strange new hairdo.

"Reading Around the World" and "Reading Rocks!" are two literacy promotion activities that encourage reading practice by recognizing the amount of time children spend reading rather than the number of pages covered. In the first strategy, the child, class, or school travels graphically around the world with each after-school hour of reading logged, charting a thousand miles for each hour. Maps, time zones, and pictures display hour milestones. The second strategy is a home-reading procedure that recognizes the amount of time parents and children spend reading silently together. Fifteen minutes per day are allotted for family reading sessions, with both the adult and child signing verification sheets. When the home team, class, or school reaches significant quantities of reading time, celebrations are held.

Baumann (1995) has named a similar program "The Millionaire's Club." She hypothesizes that if every child in a school reads for 20 or 30 minutes after school, the total number of minutes that would be read in seven or eight months, in most schools, would equal about one million minutes, explaining the name of the club. To institutionalize such a plan, Baumann suggests that teachers send letters to parents informing them of the program and asking for their assistance in seeing that their children do the required silent reading. Then a school-wide assembly can be planned, involving parents, children, and community members, to create an enthusiastic spirit as the school launches the idea of meeting the million-minute target within seven months, or whatever calculations fit the size of the school. Parents are provided with reading lists that are appropriate to the age, interests, and reading level of their child. Each class takes a field trip to the local library, where the librarian explains services and resources. After punch and cookies, each child receives his or her own gift-wrapped library card. Weekly forms are provided for each child. These forms are used for parents to record the amount of time their child read at home and the kinds of books or other reading materials the child read. Children submit the forms on Monday morning: by Tuesday, ongoing statistics regarding the number of minutes read are fed into a computer spreadsheet (older students can be taught to do this) and then reported by class, grade level, and school. A thermometer chart, entitled "Reading Is a Riot at [name of school]" is designed by children and used to record the most recent figures. The colorful chart is prominently displayed in the front entrance of the school.

Family incentives can also be used to promote silent reading. Many families have an established silent reading time, when the television is turned off, the telephone is taken off the hook, and all family members read silently. Similarly, one family initiated a Friday night Read-in-Bed policy. Much like the school Read In described earlier, the children were allowed to stay up as late as they wished, with two caveats: they must stay in bed and they must be reading. Such practices can be shared with families via a class newsletter that offers suggestions to parents about how to get their children to read at home.

Communicating with Parents About Fluency

A weekly or bimonthly class newsletter, either electronic or on paper, can be one of the most effective links to families to communicate about literacy events in the classroom, and can offer tips to parents on effective ways to get children to read at home. Such a communication device, translated into as many languages as there are primary languages in the classroom, can explain to parents what fluency is, why it is important, and how consistent reading practice will greatly enhance fluency as well as understanding of what the child reads. Parents and children for whom English is a second language should be encouraged to read together in their home language.

Another use of the class newsletter can be to match books to readers, arguably one of the most important tasks a teacher can perform. At the beginning of the year, the teacher can amass a variety of books (garage sales and book clubs are cost-effective ways to do this), making sure that they cross genres and difficulty levels so that all children can find something that appeals to them, yet providing enough variety that children become accustomed to a number of different text structures. Teachers can send home, with each child, two books that are at the child's independent reading level and that are also of interest to the child, according to the results of each child's reading interest inventory. In the class newsletter, the families can be asked, first, to read the books themselves to further help in determining which ones would be of interest to their child, and then to see that their child reads one of the books, for a few minutes each day. The parents can be given tips about discussing the books with the child through the use of nonevaluative, open-ended questions, such as:

Why do you think . . . ?

How did you feel when . . . ?

What would you have done if . . . ?

Who does [the main character] remind you of? In what way(s)?

Many other tips that promote reading fluency at home can be offered to parents. First, parents need to be informed of the importance of reading fluency and told that abundant practice reading at home, in English or in the family's home language, will contribute to fluency occurring more smoothly and rapidly. Teachers can tell parents about the pervasiveness—and the importance—of environmental print and how to call it to their children's attention at every opportunity. Teachers can tell parents about appropriate magazines for children that would make excellent birthday and special holiday gifts (the school librarian can offer the names of appropriate titles for each grade level). Teachers can suggest that model airplanes and other toys that must be assembled are excellent incentives that demand that children carefully read, reread, and follow written directions. Teachers can also encourage parents to invite their children to help them cook by reading and following simple written recipes. Finally, teachers can explain to parents how a "treasure hunt" can be a motivational way for children to read a series of directions written on small slips of paper leading from one household location to another, with the final slip of paper leading to a small prize or after-school snack.

Recorded Texts

Another way parents can promote fluency at home is through recorded texts. Listening to a recorded story on tape or CD, while also reading, allows a child to listen to the words of the text being spoken while simultaneously seeing those words on the printed page. Research has shown that this strategy enables children to increase their overall fluency, comprehension, and word-identification abilities (Opitz & Rasinski, 1998), and the modeling of the cadence of the English language is especially helpful for the second-language learners.

Commercial tapes and CDs of books written by famous people that most children admire are available. The advantage of these commercial recordings is that they are created in studios by professional story tellers and contain motivational sound effects and clear signals that let the reader know when it is time to turn the page. Also to consider, the teacher and children can make tapes cheaply with a small tape recorder. However, teachers must ensure that the reader making the tape is an exemplary reader in terms of reading expression and prosody. Parents and children may do the same at home, or, if the household has a home computer, they can record their own text at home using an inexpensive blank CD or DVD. The advantage of these homemade recordings is that most children enjoy the personal touch of a text that is made especially for them, and the speed of the reading can be adapted to the needs of the listener.

Closed-Caption Television

For many years, teachers have exhorted parents to turn off the television and, instead, encourage their children to read. While this is, in general, good advice, teachers know it is too often a losing battle. Fortunately, there is now some good news: Closed-caption television, which uses written subtitles, can provide children with meaningful and motivating reading material. Furthermore, some captioned videos, such as the Reading Rainbow program, can be purchased from video stores or educational publishers. Captioned programs can be videotaped from television, but copyright laws restrict the amount of time they can be saved and the number of times the tapes can be used (Tompkins, 2004).

As with recorded texts, several researchers (Neuman & Koskinen, 1992; Koskinen, Wilson, Gambrell, & Neuman, 1993) have found that closed-caption television is an effective way to increase fluency in a motivational way, especially for children for whom English is a second language, because the words on the screen are contextualized by the actions on the screen. Information about closed-caption television should be shared with parents. Encourage them to turn on the captioning feature that is found on most newer sets sold in the United States. Parents can be cautioned to select high-interest television programs carefully, record and preview them before making the final selections, and then introduce them to children, occasionally stopping the program at appropriate points to ask children to make predictions about what they think will happen next. Both the auditory portion and the closed captioning should be played simultaneously to provide support to children with fluency problems, helping them in their initial attempts to read. Listening to the dialogue on the television while reading the text from the captions has a reinforcing effect on the child's word recognition and reading fluency. At some later point, children should be encouraged to practice reading the captioning without the auditory portion of the program.

More information about closed-caption television programs and videos can be obtained by contacting The National Captioning Institute, 1900 Gallows Road, Suite 3000, Vienna, VA 22182.

Real World Reading Activities

Children will be more motivated to read at home when they see that reading has relevance to the outside world. Silent reading activities that show children the direct application to their lives can be planned in the classroom. Such activities are related to the "pragmatics" of language and literacy, or the use of language in a meaningful way. The instructions for these activities (adapted from Cecil & Gipe, 2003) can be given at school, while the research and reading required can be accomplished at home, with some assistance from the adults or older siblings in the child's life.

BIKE REPAIR (Grades 4–6). For this activity, the teacher or parent must acquire a number of bicycle repair manuals and lend them to children. The children are then instructed to find a broken bicycle by asking around their neighborhood or contacting a local bicycle dealer or repair shop. Then, by reading over the directions a number of times (an authentic purpose for repeated reading!), the children must determine what is wrong with the bicycle and repair it by following the instructions in the manual. (Tools, such as hammer, steel wool, wrench, oil, screwdriver, and pliers, should be made available by the repair shop or donated to the teacher by an automobile or bicycle repair shop.) Children can give weekly updates on their progress via classroom discussions. A related activity is to have children locate and review pamphlets on local and national biking groups and to share the contents of bicycle enthusiasts' magazines.

ANIMAL FACTS (Grades 2–4). This activity requires children to select an animal or insect about which most children know very little, such as the lightning bug, hammerhead shark, praying mantis, or koala bear. Children are then challenged to find as many facts about the animal or insect as they can, using books, encyclopedias, magazines, or the Internet. All research must be done outside of school. (Children who do not have a computer should be urged to visit their local library.) On a date specified by the teacher, children may share their facts with the rest of the class in a quiz-like, question-and-answer format.

CAREER QUEST (Grades 4–6). This activity will not only show children how reading can be important for finding information, but can also ignite burgeoning interest in a future career. Children tell the teacher what career they aspire to when they grow up. Then, at home, they are to find as much information as they can about that career, by using the Internet, books, and other sources and by writing letters to people who they know have such careers. After reading and rereading the information they have found, the children return to class on a date specified by the teacher. Optionally, and if appropriate, they may dress and act in the role of a person in their selected career; for example, if the child has selected the career of television reporter, he would come dressed in a sports coat and tie. Other children in the class would then ask the child questions about the career and the child would answer, in character, from his researched understandings.

ENVIRONMENTAL PRINT (Grades K–3). Parents of primary-aged young-sters can be urged to help their children gain fluency by reading the signs, posters, and other written material in their neighborhood environment. Children can be asked to read menus in restaurants, look for street names when riding in a car or on the bus, decode the names of stores, and read posters full of information about upcoming events. Repeated recognition of such environmental print will increase reading fluency.

SUMMARY

Whether the choice is Harry Potter or Captain Underpants, whether Junie B. Jones or *The Secret Garden,* one cannot possibly predict what kinds of reading material will actual-ly turn a child on to reading. We do know that the children who read the most tend to become the most fluent readers, and that the fluent readers feel successful and so tend to read even more, perpetuating the cycle. This phenomenon should send a clear signal to teachers: If we are to compete with video games, MTV, and Saturday morning cartoons, our classrooms must be stocked with an abundance of motivational reading material and time set aside for self-selected reading. Giving children the opportunity to make their own choices in reading materi-al is a big step toward promoting interest, voluntary reading, and, thus, increased fluency and getting meaning from print. It is also a cultural imperative that choices be offered that respect and acknowledge the diversity in today's classrooms.

This chapter offered two ways to provide children with the practice they need to become fluent readers who have energy in reserve to spend constructing meaning from the printed page. The first way is by provid-ing time in school during which children can read, uninterrupted, the materials they have chosen. The second approach is by finding ways to encourage children to read at home. Teachers can do this by using intrin-sic rewards, such as praising efforts and showing children real-world reasons for reading. They can also jump-start a love for reading by using extrinsic rewards, such as in-school incentives. By also using incentives offered by companies in the community, teachers can help children begin a life-long habit of recreational reading. Finally, when teachers inform the families of specific motivational activities they can use at home to encourage reading, the parents can truly become collaborators in the lit-eracy process.

REFERENCES

Anderson, R. C. (1990). *Teachers and independent reading.* Champaign-Urbana, IL: Center for the Study of Reading.

Armbruster, B. B., Lehr, F., & Osborn, J. (2000). *Put reading first: The research building blocks for teaching children to read. Kindergarten through grade 3.* Washington, DC: National Institute for Literacy.

Baumann, N. (1995). Reading millionaires—It works! *The Reading Teacher, 48,* 730–734.

Birchall, B. (1990). *Kahu, the Cautious Kiwi.* Auckland, New Zealand: Golden Press.

Burns, P. C., Roe, B. D., & Ross, E. P. (1999). *Technology for literacy learning: A primer.* Boston: Houghton Mifflin.

Cecil, N. L., & Gipe, J. P. (2003). *Literacy in the intermediate grades.* Scottsdale, AZ: Holcomb Hathaway.

Cunningham, A. E., & Stanovich, K. E. (1998). What reading does for the mind. *American Educator, 22,* 8–15.

Fielding, L. G., & Pearson, P. D. (1994). Reading comprehension: What works. *Educational Leadership, 2,* 62–68.

Guthrie, J. T., & McCann, A. D. (1997). Characteristics of classrooms that promote motivation and strategies for learning. In J. T. Guthrie & A. Wigfield (Eds.), *Reading engagement: Motivating readers through integrated instruction* (pp. 128–148). Newark, DE: International Reading Association.

Juel, C. (1988). Learning to read and write: A longitudinal study of fifty-four children from first to fourth grades. *Journal of Educational Psychology, 80,* 437–447.

Koskinen, P., Wilson, R., Gambrell, L., & Neuman, S. (1993). Captioned video and vocabulary learning: An innovative practice in literacy instruction. *The Reading Teacher, 47,* 38–43.

Krashen, S. (1994). The case for free voluntary reading. *Canadian Modern Language Review, 30,* 72–81.

Lepper, M. R., Greene, D., & Nisbett, R. E. (1973). Undermining children's intrinsic interest with extrinsic reward. *Journal of Personality and Social Psychology, 28,* 124–137.

McLoyd, V. C. (1979). The effects of extrinsic rewards of differential value on high and low intrinsic interest. *Child Development, 50,* 1010–1019.

National Reading Panel. (2000). *Report of the National Reading Panel: Teaching children to read.* Bethesda, MD: National Institute of Child Health and Human Development.

Neuman, S. B., & Koskinen, P. (1992). Captioned television as comprehensible input: Effects of incidental word learning from context for language minority students. *Reading Research Quarterly, 27*(1), 94–106.

Ohlhausen, M., & Jepson, M. (1992). Lessons from Goldilocks: "Someone has been choosing my books but I can make my own choices now!" *The New Advocate, 5,* 31–46.

Oldfather, P. (2001). *When students do not feel motivated for literacy learning: How a responsive classroom culture helps.* [Online]. Available at: http://curry.edschool.virginia.edu/go/clic/nrrc/respon_r8.html.

Opitz, M. F., & Rasinski, T. V. (1998). *Good-bye round robin: 25 oral reading strategies.* Portsmouth, NH: Heinemann.

Shanahan, T. (2002, November 7). *A sin of the second kind: The neglect of fluency instruction and what we can do about it.* PowerPoint presentation presented at A Focus on Fluency Forum, San Francisco, CA.

Stanovich, K. E. (1986). Matthew effects in reading: Some consequences of individual differences in the acquisition of literacy. *Reading Research Quarterly, 21,* 360–407.

Taylor, B. M., Pearson, P. D., Clark, K. F., & Walpole, S. (1999). *Beating the odds in teaching children to read.* (CIERA Rep. No. 2-006). Ann Arbor, MI: Center for the Improvement of Early Reading Achievement.

Tompkins, G. E. (2004). *Literacy for the 21st century: A balanced approach* (3rd ed.). Upper Saddle River, NJ: Merrill Prentice Hall.

Turner, J. (1995). The influence of classroom contexts on young children's motivation for literacy. *Reading Research Quarterly, 30,* 410–441.

Valeri-Gold, M. (1995). Uninterrupted sustained silent reading is an authentic method for developmental learners. *Journal of Reading, 38*(5), 385–386.

Weisendanger, K. D., & Birlem, E. D. (1984). The effectiveness of SSR: An overview of the research. *Reading Horizons, 24*(3), 197–201.

Willis, J. W., Stephens, E. C., & Matthew, K. I. (1996). *Technology, reading, and language arts.* Boston: Allyn & Bacon.

Worthy, J., & Broaddus, K. (2002). Fluency beyond the primary grades: From group performance to silent, independent reading. *The Reading Teacher, 55,* 334–343.

Yopp, R. H., & Yopp, H. K. (2003). Time with text. *The Reading Teacher, 57*(3), 284–287.

Fostering Writing Fluency 7

luency in writing, as well as in reading, should be a fundamental goal of every literacy program, as the two literacy processes are synergistic in nature. Writers, through their thinking and problem solving, learn about both writing and reading and how they are connected (Shanahan, 1988); also, improvement in one tends to ensure improvement in the other.

Writing goes hand in hand with reading, because writing always includes some reading during production, and reading always involves interpretation of written symbols. Through writing, a child develops strategies to hear sounds in words and to use visual cues to monitor and check her reading (Wasik, 1998). Early writers, through their rich experimentation, also learn about the conventions of print, including the fact that text carries meaning, that reading and writing text (in English) goes from left to right and top to bottom, and that a word is composed of letters and is surrounded by white space.

Writers of all ages learn how to think like authors, which helps them as they read and evaluate what other authors have written. Moreover, writers learn the importance of using just the right word or sentence to communicate their intended meaning. This way of thinking about words and sentences also applies to reading. Thus a strong focus on writing is an important component of literacy programs—especially for children who are struggling with reading (Rasinski & Padak, 2000).

Fluent writers are those who enjoy writing enough to work through successive drafts, who craft their pieces with ease, are rarely at a loss for ideas, possess a command of the conventions of writing, and have the confidence to share their products with others. To create such writers, teachers must involve children with the deepest places of their minds, their worlds, and their hearts. In order to become fluent writers, children must continually practice writing. In order to become motivated to perform the necessary practice that they need, children must be able to connect their writing to their lives: to communicate with words that are created by real feelings—not just by those that are comfortable for teachers to accept.

This chapter will offer teachers a variety of activities that encourage and develop writing fluency as well as a positive attitude toward writing. Specifically, the chapter will focus on developing the components that comprise fluent writing: the *speed* with which children write, the generating of *ideas* that motivate them to write, and the *automaticity* of the conventions of writing—spelling in particular—that allow them independence and confidence when drafting their ideas. The chapter begins with a summary of the writing process and is then divided into three sections, matching the three components of writing fluency. Each section contains suggestions that are appropriate for both the concerns of early writers and the needs of older, or more advanced, writers.

THE WRITING PROCESS

I n recent years, there has been extensive research on writing and the teaching of writing. Because of what has been learned, the emphasis in writing instruction has shifted from "product" to the "process" of writing. Teachers who are current in their understanding of the research have expanded their teaching role to include facilitator of writing and member of the classroom writing community, working right alongside the children to improve writing fluency by emphasizing the "journey of writing" rather than simply a single-draft product (Solley, 2000). We now know that fluent writers, from first-graders to professional authors, follow a similar process of crafting when they write. Teachers need to understand the components of this process in order to help each child learn and use effective writing strategies. The components of the writing process as they pertain to writing fluency—prewriting, drafting, revising, editing, and publishing—are outlined below.

Prewriting

Prewriting strategies help children generate ideas for writing and determine what they know and need to know about the topic they choose. Fluent writers have confidence that they have much to say. Therefore, they are able to tap the preponderance of ideas they are eager to share with the world. The disfluent writer needs help getting ideas.

During the prewriting phase, the author identifies the intended audience and the purpose for writing, and "rehearses," in some way, for the writing that is about to take place. This preparation may include reading a book or collecting information from several sources. Writers of all ages and ability levels benefit greatly from oral rehearsals—talking about their topic with other writers who show interest, ask them questions, and help them think about how they can communicate what they want to say in written form.

Drafting

Drafting is a tentative process, a first try that children should not perceive as producing a finished product. During this early stage in writing, the teacher/facilitator should encourage children to concentrate first on communicating their message and "to spell and punctuate as they think best" (Allen, Brown, & Yatvin, 1986, p. 463). Overemphasis on the conventions of writing, especially at the start, often interferes with the act of writing down the ideas that students are trying to express, especially for disfluent writers (Searfoss, 1993). Fluent writers seldom worry about correct language conventions (i.e., spelling, punctuation, capitalization, and paragraphing) until they are ready to edit their work; struggling writers need to be coached by the teacher to get their ideas down first and worry about the polishing later.

Revising

Revising means, literally, "seeing again." In this phase, the writer looks with fresh eyes at the writing and makes substantive changes, as needed. As writers become more fluent, they are better able to add, delete, or rearrange information to make their writing more closely match their intent. Revision is often motivated by inviting authors to share their drafts with individuals or groups who ask them questions, thus urging authors to view their writing from the audience's perspective. More fluent writers become adept at looking at their writing objectively and asking themselves the necessary questions to express their thoughts more clearly and effectively.

Editing

Editing is the final step in preparing a final draft, and it involves paying attention to the mechanics of writing, such as spelling and punctuation. Editing does not necessarily mean that the child's draft will eventually be totally error-free; instead, editing decisions should be guided by each child's evolving literacy development and corresponding ability to complete these tasks. Children take increased responsibility for proofreading and editing as they gain fluency and maturity. In the beginning (late kindergarten and first grade), the teacher or another skilled writer (a parent, teacher aide, or older child) models much of the editing for the child when a piece is being prepared for publication, thinking aloud through the process that fluent writers follow. Children are gradually taught to proofread, using editing checklists (see Exhibit 7.1) or working with peers, as they become capable of doing so. To develop editing fluency, teachers must help writers steadily improve their ability to edit independently, without overwhelming them. Children should edit a piece of writing independently, as much as they possibly can in terms of their current developmental level. If the piece is to be published, the teacher models the completion of the job for them, just as occurs with professional authors.

Publishing

Knowing that they will have a chance to bring their writing to life in front of an audience goes a long way toward motivating children to do the amount of writing that is necessary for them to become truly fluent writers. When they share their writing with audiences composed of classmates, other students, parents, or even the community, children begin to think of themselves as real authors. Fluent writers, because of their more rapid composing, are able to experience this "reward phase" proportionately more often than disfluent writers.

exhibit 7.1 Editing checklist, upper elementary.

Author:		Piece:	Editor:

AUTHOR   **EDITOR**

AUTHOR	EDITOR	
○	○	1. I have used the spelling strategies I know.
○	○	2. I have circled words I am not sure how to spell.
○	○	3. I have made sure that all sentences begin with capital letters.
○	○	4. I have ended all sentences with the correct punctuation marks.
○	○	5. I have created paragraphs for sentences that are all on the same topic.

Children's writing can be published in the form of homemade hard-cover books, through various word-processing software programs, stapled construction-paper-covered booklets, magazines, laminated class anthologies, bulletin board displays, or the plastic-covered pages of photograph albums. *All* children should publish, not only because it makes them feel like real authors, but also because it emphasizes the close connection between reading and writing, and it offers them yet another authentic reason for repeated reading: to rehearse the reading of their very own piece of writing to others. Also, as Graves (1983) reminds us, publishing should not be "the privilege of the classroom elite, the future literary scholars. Rather, it is an important mode of literary enfranchisement for each child in the classroom" (p. 55).

FOSTERING WRITING SPEED

To become fluent writers, children must be able to form letters rapidly and spell words automatically. Just as disfluent readers read word by word and have to decode many words, disfluent writers write slowly, word by word, and have to stop and sound out the spelling of many words. In fact, some disfluent writers write so slowly that by the time they get to the end of a sentence, they have forgotten what it is they are writing! Through varied, daily writing activities, children develop the fine-muscle control to form letters quickly and legibly. Through writing activities, they write high-frequency words over and over until the words become part of their sight vocabulary and they are able to spell them automatically.

Speedwriting

Speedwriting, also known as free writing and a form of quickwrites, is designed to alleviate writers' anxieties about penmanship and the correctness of language conventions in drafts (Norton, 1993).

activity

Speedwriting

The following is an exercise for speedwriting in class.

PROCEDURE

- Tell students that they will be writing nonstop for a specified amount of time (e.g. two to five minutes).
- Instruct them that they should not be concerned with erasing, crossing out, or requesting help with spelling. Explain that the idea is that they should be relaxed when writing and should allow their ideas to flow.
- At the end of the designated writing time, ask individual students to share their writing with the class.
- Invite the listeners to ask questions and offer comments and suggestions that may help the authors clarify or further develop their work.
- As an extension to speedwriting, listeners may be invited to respond to the authors' messages in written form; for example, in one speedwriting session, a third-grade girl shared a personal narrative about her grandmother, who had recently undergone an operation and died. The other children, after hearing the sad tale, immediately responded by writing sympathy cards to the bereaved child (Gipe, 2002).

Speedwriting techniques can be used to respond to stories that have been read, but they can also be used to write about what children have been learning in science, social studies, or other content areas. The teacher reads and responds to the writing and writes the correct form of misspelled words at the bottom of the page so that children will notice the correct spellings. Sometimes, the teacher may encourage children to revise and edit their speedwriting and make a final, published copy, but the major goal is to develop writing fluency rather than to create polished compositions.

Story Retelling

Another strategy for increasing writing speed is through the written retelling of stories that have just been read to children (Adams, 1990). Creating an original piece of writing requires many different skills, but when children are asked simply to focus their attention on creating a written account of a narrative that is already familiar, all their cognitive energy can be used for fluency.

Retelling a Story

activity

The following steps can be used to initiate a story retelling.

PROCEDURE

1. Read a short, engaging narrative to children, such as the book *Susan Laughs* by Jeanne Wills (Holt, 2000).
2. Stop occasionally to show and discuss the illustrations with children.
3. Using a story frame or story grammar, help children retell the story; for example:

Somebody /	wanted /	But /	So
Juan	a dog	he had allergies	His dad bought him a horse

4. Ask children to retell the story in written form, stating the time they will have to complete the task (e.g., ten minutes for primary grades; five minutes for intermediate grades). Explain that they are to write rapidly without stopping, and concentrate on retelling what happened in the story rather than focusing on the "correctness" of the writing.
5. Read and respond to the story retelling by providing comments about the content of the retelling on the top of the page and writing corrections at the bottom of the page.

GENERATING IDEAS FOR WRITING

Fluent writers seem to have a continuous flow of ideas. With such a built-in writing agenda, these writers quickly get to work on assigned writing tasks and therefore have considerably more practice than their less fluent counterparts, who spend endless time struggling to think of topics about which they can write.

Fortunately, this problem is one that can be remedied in an elementary writing class: Children simply need to be given motivational input in the form of writing "prompts," or motivational ideas, that will quickly engage them in the writing process.

Prompts

If a teacher strolls into the classroom on a warm sunny day and spontaneously asks children to write a poem about spring, the fluent writers—those who could effortlessly generate ten pages on the joy of clean sheets—will probably get straight to work. The other children, who will undoubtedly constitute the majority, will have little or nothing to say. No writing practice, so essential to writing fluency, will occur for them.

On the other hand, if the teacher provides a motivational prompt to inspire children (see Exhibit 7.2) or provides scaffolds—templates that help them to understand what they are to do—children become engaged in writing and find they have much to say. Writing ideas come when challenging directions, interesting patterns, and provoking examples open doors to thinking and expressing.

Literature can also be used to prompt ideas. For example, after the teacher reads to the children *Alexander and the Terrible, Horrible, No*

exhibit 7.2 **Motivational prompts.**

Write (about):

○ The most embarrassing/exciting thing that ever happened to you

○ A day you will always remember/you'd like to forget

○ Your best friend, or how to be one

○ If you could rule the school/world, what would you change?

○ Ten countries you would like to visit and why

○ Why an earlobe is more valuable than an elbow

○ Why you should be the next American Idol

○ 25 uses for a paper cup

○ The most important item that was ever invented

○ A dinner invitation to a cat from a mouse

○ 10 things never to say to a gorilla

○ What will happen if we don't take care of our natural resources

Good, Very Bad Day by Judith Viorst (Atheneum, 1972), he can share a very bad day that he had. Then, he can urge the children to write about a bad day that they had had or invite them to write a list of 10 things they could/should not say to someone who is having a bad day. Or a book such as *Clyde Monster* by Robert L. Crowe (E. P. Dutton, 1986) can be stopped at the most exciting point and the children urged to predict and then write about what happens next—such as when Clyde is too scared to go into his cave to sleep. Exhibit 7.3 shows some brainstormed ideas of what happens next. The children select one of the brainstormed endings, or one that has not been mentioned, and write the end of the story.

Another example is story starters, a kind of writing prompt that also ensures that writers will be able to get started with an idea. Story starters (see Exhibit 7.4) consist of a one-line provocative sentence, a picture that goes with the sentence, and six words that might go in a story emanating from the sentence. The sentences can be written and the illustrations drawn or printed on 5" x 8" cards, laminated, and placed in the classroom writing center so that children having difficulty finding a writing topic can be inspired.

Finally, children need to be given structures for expository writing and practice using them to become fluent in content-area writing. Expository

exhibit 7.3 **Brainstorming web.**

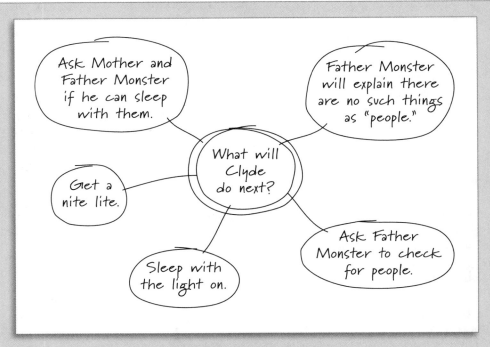

exhibit 7.4 **Sample story starter.**

> He was the tiniest little horse
> I ever saw and he was just sitting
> on my desk when I came to school
> that morning.
>
> pinto   stable
> whinnied   trotting
> hooves   mane

writing differs in purpose from narrative and descriptive writing. The intent of a narrative is to entertain by telling a story, and the purpose of a description is to present the details about a topic in a somewhat static context. Exposition, on the other hand, seeks to instruct, explain, and/or persuade. Narrative discourse (the language of literature) and expository discourse (the language of most content area textbooks) are the kind of texts that elementary school children most commonly read and write. Exhibit 7.5 offers a host of discourse formats for expository writing.

Dialogue Journals

Robert Frost, the great American poet, was reported to have said, "There is no art to writing but having something to say." Children will be eager to express themselves in writing and will have plenty to say if they believe that what they have to write about is interesting and will be read by others. One of the best ways to encourage children to tap into their own ideas is through the use of dialogue journals.

A wide range of language functions can be practiced through a written conversation that takes place between a teacher and child via a dialogue journal, where children can share their opinions and personal and general facts, respond to and ask questions, complain, confess, apologize, thank, evaluate, and promise, among other typical uses (Staton, Shuy, Peyton, & Reed, 1988). In general, children are free to write about what is of personal interest to them at that particular point in time, so ideas flow as easily as any oral conversation might. Exhibit 7.6 shows a series of entries by a child in the third grade. Note how many different purposes for writing the child has incorporated. Note, also, how the child

exhibit 7.5 **Discourse formats for content-area writing.**

Journals and diaries (real or imaginary)	Reviews: books, TV, films
Biographical sketches	Historical "you are there" scenes
Anecdotes and stories:	Science notes: observations,
from experience; told	lab reports
by others	Math: story problems, solutions
Guess who/what descriptions	to problems; record books
Letters:	Responses to literature
Personal reactions	Interviews:
Observations	Imaginary
Persuasive:	Real
To the editor	Directions: How-to
To public officials	School or neighborhood guide
Requests	Dictionaries and lexicons
Applications	Future options, notes on:
Memos	Careers, employment
Resumes and summaries	School and training
Telegrams	Written debates
Epitaphs	Taking a stand:
Editorials	School issues
Commentaries	Family problems
Response and rebuttal	State, national issues
Fact sheets	Moral questions
School newspaper items	Global problems
Proposals	Prophecies and predictions
Ballads	PowerPoint presentations

Source: Adapted from Tchudi & Tchudi, 1983.

edits her spelling in subsequent entries after the teacher has responded to her ideas using the correct spellings of words the child had used.

The functional language development provided by dialogue journal writing is essential to both reading and writing fluency in that the writer must learn to use language to facilitate a certain response in the reader. Second-language learners can obtain useful writing practice by writing in English, but they can also be encouraged to "code-switch," or write words unknown to them in English in their home language.

exhibit 7.6 **Kim's dialogue journal.**

[Teacher responds]	[Student initiates]
No, I have never been to Hawaii, Kim, but I have always wanted to go there. Did you get to do any snorkeling? Yes, I noticed your lovely tan!	We had such a fun time in ~~Howiy~~ Hawie Mrs. Cecil. Were you ever thare? I got sun bruned like a ~~lobe~~ lobstor. Did you notis Mrs. Cecil. I can't wait to go back thare.
Snorkeling is fun, isn't it, Kim? How did you learn? Did your mother teach you? Was it difficult? What else did you do in Hawaii?	Yes we got to ~~snu~~ snorkel when we were in Hawaii. It was so neat! There were so many fish with all difrint colors. I never saw anything like that befor.
I'm sorry you are being bothered, Kim. I will change your seat and speak with Meg. No, I am not angry with you! ☺	You know Mrs. Cecil. You were telling me to stop talking today in math class. but it wasn't me. Meg was talking. Meg keeps bothing me. Please move her seat. Dont be mad at me please, Mrs. Cecil??
I have one daughter, Kim. Like you, I am sure she thinks I am mean sometimes. It is hard being a Mommy!	Mrs. Cecil, do you have any children? I wish I was your child. Instead of your student. My mother is to mene. I think you are probly never mene to your children?
Kim, the important thing is that you have now told the truth. Sometimes it's hard to tell the truth. No, I am not angry, but please don't do it again, okay? ☺	Now I want to tell you something o.k. Last weak when I was absint I was'nt sick. I ~~jus~~ just made that up becuase I wanted to stay home and watch Scuby Do. Im sorry. Mrs. Cecil. Are you angry now???? Do'nt be.

Source: Cecil & Gipe (2003).

Most teachers initiate dialogue journals by asking questions for each child and then responding themselves to the child's journal entries. This is an ideal way to encourage fluent written expression without undue concern for perfection in the conventions of language. As the written conversation develops, children begin to write longer and longer entries, as they realize that the teacher is concerned with, and responding to, *what* is being said, rather than *how* it is being said. An alternate form of journals, e-mail dialogue journals, is now surfacing in classrooms as a vehicle for general correspondence or for sharing responses to literature (Sullivan, 1998).

AUTOMATICITY IN WRITING

To become "automatic" in their writing, children must have a command of the conventions of writing so they can spend more energy with their ideas than with the actual formulation of text. They must also be aware of strategies that tell them how to think through problems and concerns that all writers encounter as they are composing a piece of writing. The following sections describe how teachers can model fluent writing behavior for children and give strategies children can use when they possess limited spelling prowess, to help children develop automaticity in their writing.

Teacher Modeling of Automaticity in Writing

A comprehensive program of writing instruction should provide daily demonstrations and mini-lessons, modeling how writers use the conventions of language and think through many different kinds of writing strategies. The teacher should also offer guided practice sessions, where children can use their new skills with the assistance of a proficient writer, and, finally, independent writing sessions where children are offered the opportunity to practice their newly acquired skills. Such sessions show children how fluent writers think through the host of writing decisions that authors must make and what they do when they discover any problems. After each session, the teacher should allow children to gain valuable practice in implementing these writing tools until they become second nature. Children can then be said to have reached the stage of automaticity in writing.

Writing Aloud, Writing TO

Writing Aloud, Writing TO (Reutzel & Cooter, 2002) is an example of a technique that can be used to model various aspects of the writing process. (The "Writing TO" part of Writing Aloud, Writing TO comes from the practice of Writing TO, WITH, and BY in a comprehensive writing program of instruction. Writing TO students refers to demonstrations and mini-lessons.) The authors of the approach offer the following suggestions:

1. The teacher chooses a writing topic, a particular writing structure, and a purpose for writing. For example, the teacher may want to teach children about writing an expository paragraph using comparison and contrast between the United States and Australia.

2. The teacher thinks aloud as he writes the paragraph, explaining explicitly what he is doing, while the children watch and listen. ("I want to talk about Australia and the United States. Since they are both different and alike, I will use a comparison and contrast format.")

3. The teacher constantly makes the connection from the spoken to the written word and sometimes asks the children to read aloud with him.

4. The teacher thinks through the process of paragraphing, punctuating, spelling, and word choice, and often asks questions to engage children in the process. ("I am making a list of ways in which the United States and Australia are similar: They both speak English, they were both once owned by England, and they both are very large countries. What punctuation marks must I use to separate these three ideas? What is another word I could use to say that a country was once owned by England? How can I find out how to spell the word 'eucalyptus'?")

SPELLING CONCERNS AND WRITING FLUENCY

Of all the conventions necessary for writing fluency and automaticity, spelling problems, especially, tend to slow down and "inhibit many students who would otherwise be imaginative, intelligent writers" (Silva & Yarborough, 1990, p. 48).

Because the purpose in this chapter is to enable children to write with fluency—and not to have them dwell on correct spelling to the detriment of that end—the strategies offered are ones that enable children to do their best to spell unknown words and then move along with their writing; the correction of any spelling errors can happen at a later, editing phase and can be ameliorated through mini-lessons designed to target children's needs at a particular spelling stage.

For the purpose of writing fluency, children need to be taught some expedient strategies that can help them figure out independently how to spell, or approximate the spelling of, unknown words. The following strategies (Cecil & Gipe, 2003) should be taught to children one at a time and then placed on a chart and posted prominently in the classroom. The children can then refer to the chart whenever they are writing and need to know how to spell a word before they can move on.

- Make an attempt: Try three spellings of the word and then choose the one that looks best to you.
- See if the word is on a word wall or other environmental print around the room.
- Think of another word you know that sounds like, or rhymes with, the word. Try spelling it like that word.
- Say the word out loud and put a letter to each sound you hear.
- If the word is long, break it into parts and spell each part.
- Look up the word in the dictionary.
- Ask someone how to spell the word.

ESPECIALLY FOR EARLY WRITERS

Beginning writers (almost all kindergarteners, many first-graders, and some second-graders) make extensive use of drawing as a prewriting activity. Young children, especially those who lack writing fluency because they have trouble thinking of ideas, often benefit by drawing as a prewriting rehearsal (Sidelnick & Svoboda, 2000). Drawing also provides opportunities for children who lack fluency because of fine-motor issues to represent what they want to write through another modality or writing system that is more accessible than print. Drawing, therefore, should be accepted and encouraged as a path to writing fluency for early writers.

Allowing for Developmental Differences

It is critical for teachers to respond to the writing of young children, regardless of form, as "meaningful messages" (Adams, 1990). Like reading, writing develops for young children in an environment where they see its functional use frequently modeled by adults, where inviting materials and the time to use them are readily available, and where experimental print is not only accepted but also actively encouraged by the teacher. Especially with kindergarteners, who vary in their ability to create readable print, the teacher must make the effort to ask the child about the meaning of her message, whatever form it may take.

As an example, one kindergarten teacher models writing by gathering young children around her and soliciting a short message from the children, such as, "I am hoping we will have burritos for lunch." She explains that there are various ways to create this message, beginning with a crude picture of a burrito. She then produces some scribble writing and runs her hand from left to right under the writing, while reading the message. She explains that, while it looks like cursive writing, it is a special kind of kindergarten writing called "scribble writing." She continues to show the children other ways writing can appear, as she uses letter strings, phonemic writing, and finally conventional writing, always carefully validating the message by reading it from left to right. In this way, young children feel free to practice creating messages at their own developmental level without undue concern with "correctness," which often interferes with the spontaneous flow of their wonderfully original ideas.

Interactive Writing

Interactive writing, or shared writing, is a writing activity in which children and the teacher come together to create a text on chart paper (Button, Johnson, & Furgerson, 1996). The teacher is the facilitator as the children write the text they compose, word by word, on the chart. Children take turns writing the words and letters they know, adding punctuation marks, and using their fingers to make the appropriate spaces between the words. The teacher guides the children to spell all the words correctly and to use the other mechanics properly so that the text is easily readable. Besides participating in the writing of the text on the chart, children sometimes have their own personal white boards, on which they copy the message. This interactive writing provides children with the guided writing practice that they need in order to achieve automaticity in writing. It also offers the following advantages (Tompkins, 2004):

- It allows children to practice writing high-frequency words.
- It allows the teacher to model phonics and spelling strategies.
- It offers children the opportunity to write text that they could not do independently.
- It provides children a vehicle through which to share their writing fluency with their classmates.

Morning Message

Teachers can also write interactively with young children by using a combination of modeling and shared writing to produce the *morning message* (Kawakami-Arakaki, Oshiro, & Farran, 1989). Typically, the teacher, in a short (five to seven minutes) session, writes about what will be happening that day in terms of schedule or activities, or about what has been occurring in the teacher's or children's lives. A morning message is inherently motivational and provides an excellent opportunity for children to learn about writing fluency as they assist the teacher in modeling new words and conventions of print. Exhibit 7.7 shows an example of a morning message.

exhibit 7.7 **Example of a morning message.**

> Today is Tuesday, November 17. It is rainy and windy outside. The temperature is 48 degrees. LaToya is our classroom helper. Today we are going to have burritos for lunch. It is computer day and we will go to the computer lab at 10:00 and finish writing our stories. At 1:30 our sixth-grade reading buddies will come to our classroom. They will read a story with us. Our student teacher, Ms. Cherie, went back to the university. Yesterday was her last day. We will miss her!

SUMMARY

Writing is important in the development of fluency because reading and writing are reciprocal processes in the development of literacy; by improving one, you automatically improve the other. In order to become fluent writers, children need to believe that they have important things to say. They should be surrounded by stimulating ideas and encouraged to create their own from their personal life stories. Children become fluent by being shown how to write by proficient writers and then being given plenty of opportunities to emulate what they have been shown and taught. Given ample practice with the underlying skills of writing, they will eventually incorporate them and reach a level of writing automaticity. Such practice also increases the speed with which they are able to go through the writing process in order to bring their thoughts to fruition. They then are able to experience the heady exhilaration of publishing—a just reward for work well done.

REFERENCES

Adams, M. J. (1990). *Beginning to read: Thinking and learning about print.* Cambridge, MA: The MIT Press.

Allen, R., Brown, K., & Yatvin, J. (1986). *Learning language through communication: A functional perspective.* Belmont, CA: Wadsworth.

Button, K., Johnson, M. J., & Furgerson, P. (1996). Interactive writing in a primary classroom. *The Reading Teacher, 49,* 446–454.

Cecil, N. L., & Gipe, J. P. (2003). *Literacy in the intermediate grades: Best practices for a comprehensive program.* Scottsdale, AZ: Holcomb Hathaway.

Gipe, J. P. (2002). *Multiple paths to literacy: Classroom techniques for struggling readers.* Upper Saddle River, NJ: Merrill Prentice Hall.

Graves, D. (1983). *Writing: Teachers and children at work.* Portsmouth, NH: Heinemann.

Kawakami-Arakaki, A., Oshiro, M., & Farran, S. (1989). Research to practice: Integrating reading and writing in a kindergarten curriculum. In J. Mason (Ed.), *Reading and writing connections* (pp. 199–218). Boston: Allyn & Bacon.

Norton, D. (1993). *The effective teaching of language arts,* 4th ed. New York: Merrill.

Pinnell, G. S., & Fountas, I. C. (1998). *Word matters: Teaching phonics and spelling in the reading/writing classroom.* Portsmouth, NH: Heinemann.

Rasinski, T., & Padak, N. (2000). *Effective reading strategies: Teaching children who find reading difficult.* Upper Saddle River, NJ: Merrill Prentice Hall.

Reutzel, D. R., & Cooter, R. B. (2002). *Strategies for reading assessment and instruction: Helping every child succeed,* 2nd ed. Upper Saddle River, NJ: Merrill Prentice Hall.

Searfoss, L. (1993). Assessing classroom environments. In S. Glazer & C. Brown (Eds.), *Portfolios and beyond: Collaborative assessment in reading and writing* (pp. 11–26). Norwood, MA: Christopher-Gordon.

Shanahan, T. (1988). The reading–writing relationship: Seven instructional principles. *The Reading Teacher, 41,* 636–647.

Sidelnick, M., & Svoboda, M. (2000). The bridge between drawing and writing: Hannah's story. *The Reading Teacher, 54,* 174–184.

Silva, C., & Yarborough, B. (1990). Help for young writers with spelling difficulties. *Journal of Reading, 34,* 48–53.

Solley, B. (2000). *Writers' workshop: Reflections of elementary and middle school teachers.* Boston: Allyn & Bacon.

Staton, J., Shuy, R. W., Peyton, J. K., & Reed, L. (1988). *Dialogue journal communication: Classroom, linguistic, social and cognitive views.* Norwood, NJ: Ablex.

Sullivan, J. (1998). The electronic journal: Combining literacy and technology. *The Reading Teacher, 52,* 90–93.

Tchudi, S., & Tchudi, S. J. (1983). *Teaching writing in the content areas: Elementary school.* Washington, DC: National Education Association.

Tompkins, G. E. (2000). *Teaching writing: Balancing process and product,* 3rd ed. Upper Saddle River, NJ: Merrill Prentice Hall.

Tompkins, G. E. (2004). *Literacy in the 21st century: A balanced approach.* Upper Saddle River, NJ: Merrill Prentice Hall.

Wasik, B. (1998). Using volunteers as reading tutors: Guidelines for successful practices. *The Reading Teacher, 51,* 562–570.

Fluency and Technology 8

A major objective of an effective literacy program is to develop fluent readers. But increased fluency—as well as vocabulary, background knowledge, and comprehension—is an outcome of the amount of text that is read. The more children practice the skills of reading, the more information, motivation, and pleasure they derive. The computer can be an important tool to encourage children to read *more*. The motivational appeal of technology, which is finally finding its way into most classrooms, coupled with highly engaging literacy software, can provide valuable assistance in helping children to become more fluent readers. Moreover, in the elementary classroom, computers can become helpful aides for the activities of repeated readings, paired reading, and the modeling of fluent reading behavior. The computer is an indefatigable classroom aide and can be used by a skilled teacher to create tailor-made lessons for individual children and small groups.

Research tells us that when a passage is read repeatedly, the number of word-recognition errors decreases and reading rate increases, as does more appropriate oral reading expression (Samuels, 2002). By adding the computer to this process, teachers now have a teaching assistant that can act as a model and support for reading text quickly and accurately, and with appropriate phrasing and expression. Many software products on the market today provide a model of fluent reading, as well as plenty of patient feedback for the child; other products provide the child with ample practice for repeated readings and paired reading.

As a cautionary note, we should be careful not to use computers as substitutes for excellent instruction from a strong, diagnostic classroom teacher who can personally deliver lessons tailored to the individual needs of her students. Technology should be used as a tool and not as the curriculum itself; it should be integrated with existing curricula rather than considered just "one more subject to add to the day." Additionally, technology should always be used in such a way that children are engaged in thinking and not simply responding to entertaining cues. Indeed, Labbo and Reinking (1999) make a distinction between learning *from* a computer (skill and drill exercises) and *with* the computer in ways that stimulate children to transact with text in meaningful ways.

In this chapter, we will explore many widely used programs that can be used to promote reading fluency through the use of modeling, individual repeated readings, and interactive reading and writing. Although many other software programs are available for the same purposes (see Appendix C), the ones chosen for this chapter are prototypes of computer activities that allow children to learn *with*, not simply *from*, the computer. They are also worthy examples of activities that allow children to increase their fluency in a joyful literacy context.

CHOOSING SOFTWARE

Technology should not be used merely for its own sake, simply because it is *there*. Any technology use should support or add value to the literacy goals that the teacher has already established.

Moreover, the teacher must be familiar with the available software programs and how to integrate them effectively with the currently used literacy curriculum. Finally, the software must be developmentally appropriate in order for it to have an impact on children's learning. Reviews of educational software are available online at www.superkids.com. Additionally, keep in mind the following suggestions when choosing software (adapted from Labbo, Leu, Kinzer, et al., 2003):

- Does the program serve the intended purpose? For example, if it purports to improve fluency, can I see that children's fluency is actually improving?
- Can the software program be used independently by my students, or will I need to be present to facilitate?
- Are there so many sight and sound distractions that children will become overstimulated and lose the literacy focus?
- Does the computer software program offer children an opportunity for free choice? (This can be part of the motivation for using technology.)
- Does the computer program use humor? Children tend to prefer these programs and use them more frequently.
- Does the software program align with conventional literacy goals, district benchmarks, and state standards for literacy?
- Does the program address my students' individual fluency needs?
- Does the program contribute to an overall unit theme or project?

INTERACTIVE READING AND WRITING: ELECTRONIC BOOKS

Fluency can be enhanced in an enjoyable social context using paired reading—with children doing several readings of the same text and offering feedback to one another—as described in Chapter 5. Electronic books (e-books) on CD-ROM can play a similar role, and they may be instrumental in improving automatic word recognition and providing a "digital language experience approach," reinforcing fluency and the link between written and oral language (Labbo, Eakle, & Montero, 2002).

These electronic books offer children the ability to self-select the amount of assistance they want, thus increasing individual control over the learning environment as they choose for themselves where and when they need help (Leu, 1997). For example, when children come to a word or phrase they do not know, they can click on the text to have the computer read it for them, removing the burden of decoding (McKenna, 1998) and allowing for more fluent reading on subsequent attempts.

Ultimately, the children have more energy to consider the meaning of—and to reap enjoyment from—the text.

A further use of electronic books is to help the teacher differentiate instruction and provide a wider range of opportunities for all children to interact with text. As all teachers know, children develop their literacy skills at their own rate, in their own time frames. Most teachers deal with children on many different developmental reading levels. While the same level of basal reader is often used to teach all the children in a class, teachers can benefit from books on CD-ROM as valuable alternative resources to engage children in successful reading at all levels (McKenna, 1998).

Although considerable differences exist in the variety of features offered by electronic books, almost all contain audio and graphic animations that allow the characters to talk and seemingly come to life through the use of "hotspots" that produce animation, sound effects, or other features when a child clicks on them. Most also invite children to highlight an unfamiliar phrase or listen to a reader pronounce a word for them (Lefever-Davis & Pearman, 2005). Some electronic storybooks will read the entire book aloud for children, providing an individualized read-aloud with which the child or children can track along using the mouse.

The Reader Rabbit Series

Widely used examples of electronic "books" are those in the Reader Rabbit series (The Learning Company, 1996; see Exhibit 8.1). These electronic books use digitalized pronunciations of certain words and sentences to aid in reading accuracy. The child may opt to have the entire story read aloud, offering her a model of fluent reading while she tracks along. On most illustrations, *hot spots,* which the child can choose to click on, cause characters to speak, animals to make appropriate sounds, and objects to move or make sounds. In this program, some hot spots are activated automatically. Most children find the stories enjoyable and are delighted by the fact that the characters seem to come to life, but teachers should use them judiciously, ensuring that children are actively reading. Certain children find the hot spots distracting, or they take a passive stance and expect to be entertained by the books (Lefever-Davis & Pearman, 2005). If this happens, teachers should discard the computer program in favor of a more interactive book that encourages the child to take a more active stance.

Illuminatus 4.5

One multimedia authoring program, Illuminatus 4.5 (1999), can be used by pairs of children working collaboratively to create their own electronic talking books (Oakley, 2002). The program can teach children to self-monitor

exhibit 8.1 **Reader Rabbit series, a widely used series of electronic books.**

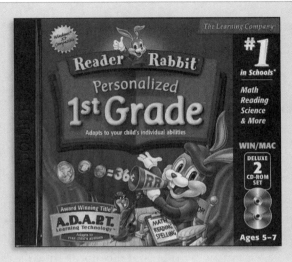

their oral reading for fluency—appropriate rate, smoothness, and expression—and to think about phrasing as they work together to create and highlight written text to accompany their oral narration of their writing.

Using this program, the children can first be introduced to several electronic talking books, such as *Just Me and My Dad* (Meyer, 1996) or *Arthur's Teacher Troubles* (1993). They then make their own talking book by creating a series of sketches of each page or screen, or a kind of "story board" that shows the pictures and the text. They also have to decide on what interactive effects there would be; for example, if a user clicks on a certain picture, what sounds or animation would occur?

Pairs of children then take turns acting as "scribe" and keying their story into Illuminatus, which contains a word-processing program, with which most children are familiar. After finishing the typing, the children record the narration of their story. The children practice their reading several times during the recording, and they are able to hear the replays and to see wave patterns, or "waveforms," on the screen, corresponding to their pitch and volume (see Exhibit 8.2 for an example).

The audio recordings and wave patterns prompt discussions between the children about what fluent reading should sound (and look) like, and, with initial teacher modeling and guidance, children may offer each other insightful observations about appropriate intonation, volume, pronunciation, and phrasing. The children usually record their narrations several times before they are happy with the sound and the "look," providing authentic opportunities for repeated readings. Teachers often report that

exhibit 8.2 Waveforms.

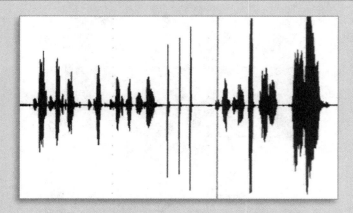

pairs of children are amused by their narrations as they listen to them, and they seem to agree when a piece of text has not been read fluently. Instead of being embarrassed by disfluent reading, children tend to refer to such patches as "bloopers," and immediately rerecord the text (Oakley, 2002).

Start-to-Finish™

Another example of electronic books is provided by the Start-to-Finish™ (Start-to-Finish Publishing Company, 2000) library of electronic books. This program combines a computer book, an audiocassette, and a paperback book to scaffold a reading experience for older, struggling readers so they can successfully transition from reading with computer assistance to independently reading text. Using this program, older children are motivated to read content that is appropriate to their interests because they can follow the highlighted text as it is read by a proficient reader in digitalized, recorded speech. As with the electronic books discussed earlier, this program lessens frustration for struggling readers because children can hear every single unfamiliar word with a single click of the mouse.

Guidelines for Choosing Electronic Books

The following are some helpful guidelines for choosing electronic books to use in fostering reading fluency (adapted from Tompkins, 2005):

- Select programs that contain high-quality children's literature.
- Determine that the books are engaging enough to encourage repeated readings.

- Be sure that the electronic book is interactive and offers assistance when children cannot decode a word.
- Check that the graphics with animations are not so dense or distracting that they slow the reading process.
- Select books that allow active, rather than passive, interaction.
- Always choose books that are appropriate for the children's interest level and at their instructional reading levels.

SUPPLEMENTAL PROGRAMS FOCUSING ON REPEATED READINGS

Several complete reading programs on the market today are based on current scientific research on reading fluency. These programs do not offer computer feedback or modeling; their approach is more traditional, although the computer is used to motivate children to read. The programs also provide useful tools for teacher record keeping.

Read Naturally

One of the most widely used of these programs is Read Naturally (Davidson, 2003). The entire package includes books, tapes, CDs, and software programs. Its approach offers guided oral repeated reading and repeated-reading techniques, as well as concomitant quantitative feedback. The repeated reading, although not for authentic purposes, emerges from goal rates set collaboratively by the child and teacher. The program also provides the Reading Fluency Monitor, a system for monitoring children's progress and a useful assessment tool for periodic screening, assessment, and progress monitoring from grade 1 through grade 8.

Read Naturally begins with a placement procedure to make sure that children will work at the appropriate text reading level. Once the placement has been determined, the children select a story from their prescribed level and locate the tape or CD for the story. Before actually reading, the children use the story's title, pictures, and key words to write a sentence predicting what the story will be about. After writing a prediction, the children read the story aloud, timing themselves for one minute, and underlining any unknown words. They then record on a graph, in blue, the number of words they read correctly in the one-minute timing. In the next step, they read along with the tape three times, tracking and subvocalizing with the audiotape.

Practice continues with the children reading the story without the audiotape until they can read at or above the predetermined rate goal agreed upon by the teacher and the child. Each practice is timed. When children can read at or above the predetermined rate goal, they answer comprehension questions and prepare for a timed reading with the teacher. To pass, the children must meet the reading rate goal, make fewer than three errors, read with appropriate expression, and answer the comprehension questions correctly. The fluency score is then recorded in red on the graph.

In the final step, the children retell the story either orally or in written form. Children must either include a certain number of ideas or write for a certain length of time. When children complete the last step successfully, they select a new story and begin the process again. Teachers, with input from each child, can adjust goals and reading levels at any time during the process.

Great Leaps Reading Program

Great Leaps Reading Program is a less extensive program that also uses proven instructional practices with powerful motivators to remediate a variety of reading problems. It has three components: Phonics, Sight Phrases, and Reading Fluency.

The Phonics component uses flash cards of phonemic elements to help children apply the sound/symbol relationships. The Sight Phrases component helps children to master high frequency sight words and phrases while developing and improving children's focusing skills. The Reading Fluency component has children read appropriate stories specifically designed to build reading rate, motivation, and proper intonation. The students read these stories repeatedly, charting their comprehension and fluency. Through using this program, approximately 25 percent of the children surveyed by the publishers showed from two to five years' growth in reading fluency in fewer than six months of usage.

PROGRAMS OFFERING FEEDBACK AND SUPPORT

Other computer software programs offer customized feedback and support for children who are having difficulty with fluency and need more individualized help. Through the use of state-of-the-art speech-recognition technology, such programs not only model reading for the child, they also offer feedback about the child's reading.

Soliloquy Reading Assistant

Soliloquy Reading Assistant (Soliloquy Learning, Inc., 2003) is an example of a program that can be a valuable classroom tool because it allows children to practice oral reading independently. The program offers classroom teachers a virtual classroom aide, not only modeling proficient reading for the child, but also actually "listening" to the children as they read aloud. Using sophisticated technology that actually responds to human speech, the program provides instant intervention when the child is struggling, as well as assistance with pronunciations and word meanings.

The computer software that comes with this program allows the computer to virtually "listen" to the child read out loud. The program presents the text on the computer screen, and it then "listens" to the spoken words the child reads and provides feedback and support if the child has difficulty. If the child does not know how to pronounce a word or phrase, the computer software pronounces the unfamiliar text for the child. If the child doesn't know the meaning of a word, the software explains it in the exact context of the passage. Additionally, the program tracks the child's fluency and accuracy over time, offering the teacher valuable diagnostic information about the child's needs and progress (Wren, 2005).

Because the computer is essentially robotic, it has one distinct advantage over its human counterpart: It is tireless and infinitely patient. Children may sit for hours and practice reading out loud for this mechanical listener. They may even read the same story over and over, if they wish, gaining valuable fluency practice through the repeated readings.

Because research indicates that spending time on the practice of reading and having opportunities for repeated oral reading are two major factors in developing reading fluency, software programs such as Soliloquy hold much promise for helping children to develop fluency at their own pace.

COMPUTER PROGRAMS TO
ENHANCE WRITING FLUENCY

Children become fluent writers when they are given many opportunities to practice writing. Landauer (1995) captured the potential of computers as tools for writing when he described the computer as being capable of offering a kind of "power tool for the human mind" (p. 137). By removing the small-motor concerns associated with writing in longhand, computers used for writing and composing have the exciting capacity to enhance and extend their users' abilities to create and produce their ideas more fluently.

One can choose from a variety of computer tools, and, when used in certain ways, each of these tools has the potential to support writing fluency development. Writing also requires repeated reading, and word processors provide an interesting alternative interface in which students can experience text. Using the computer, children can compose more rapidly as they construct knowledge by creating reports and stories using word-processing programs and computer graphics, and presentations using applications such as KidPix (Riverdeep, 2005) and PowerPoint. Expressing knowledge through stories, reports, or slideshows requires thinking about the important ideas involved in a concept and then skimming and scanning through resources to find material that supports the concepts or arguments the students are attempting to make.

A variety of word-processing programs, desktop publishing programs, and graphics packages support children who are involved in a writer's workshop (Cochran-Smith, 1991; Tompkins, 2005). Some of the most suitable for increasing writing fluency are Kid Works II, Kidwriter Gold, and Mac Write Pro. Children can revise and edit their rough drafts much more easily when they use these word-processing programs, and they can then print out neat, final copies without the "busy work" of constant recopying that I recall from my own laborious pre–word processing days! With desktop publishing, children can create professional-looking newspapers, pamphlets, and even books for class. Because of the ease of the physical act of writing, children who are proficient at word processing will be eager to write more prolifically. With the increased practice, increased fluency in writing naturally follows.

Using computers can also support the pursuit of constructivist strategies such as Guthrie and McCann's (1997) concept-oriented reading instruction (CORI), as described in Chapter 6. The computer provides a collaborative gathering place where peers can work together to create literacy-based products that will ultimately be of high interest to them because they have created those products. Children will not only write more fluently through practice, but they will be constantly motivated to reread what they have written. Because of these varied capacities, the wise use of computers can be extremely effective in helping to support fluency development in both reading and writing.

TOOLS TO INCREASE READING RATE

Rapid reading is but one factor in determining fluency, and slow reading can interfere with accurate phrasing and proper expression. A slow reading rate may be caused by a host of factors, including word-by-word reading, finger pointing, lip movements, subvocalization, overanalyzing words, slowness in recognizing words by sight, too many regressive eye movements, and oral-reading repetitions. Reduced reading rate can also occur when children have difficulty going from the end of one line to the beginning of the next (return sweep), or when they are unable to take in an adequate amount of material in one fixation of the eyes. Additional causes of slow reading rate are overuse of phonics, underdeveloped word-recognition skills, inability to adjust rate for differing purposes, or vision problems that have not been properly diagnosed. Before the following technological tools are used with children, it is suggested that the underlying causes for the slow reading be diagnosed and treated.

The following technological devices were designed for the purpose of increasing reading rate. In some cases, no actual text is provided and words are presented to children in isolation, as compared with the programs described earlier in the chapter that offer complete literacy lessons. Such exercises, in moderation, may help children to recognize words more quickly and break ingrained habits such as spending too long laboring over the pronunciation of one word; however, these exercises lack the personal meaning—and thus enjoyment—of authentic reading activities and should therefore be used advisedly and sparingly.

AceReader

The AceReader (AceReader, 2005) is a "tachistoscopic device," which means that it projects a series of images onto a computer screen at rapid speed to test visual perception, memory, and word recognition. It helps children learn to read faster by scrolling text from computer documents or an electronic clipboard, while accurately tracking user speed and progress. AceReader options include set font, set background color, set mode (Center Text or Eye Trainer Scroll), number of words or lines per flash, column width, set delays (if certain punctuation or long words are found), and lengths of the exposure time.

Reading Speed Drills

Reading Speed Drills (Oxton House) contain computer-generated word-list drills designed to promote reading rate. The drills help children develop automaticity by responding to whole words and the orthographic units of which they are composed. The program also contains contrast cards, which develop fluency by offering the correct sounds for the orthographic units. Additionally, the program includes decodable text with phonetically controlled vocabulary that uses realistic stories providing a rich resource for repeated readings, comprehension activities, and class discussions. Integrated within a context of much predictable text and high-quality children's literature, this program can help children improve their reading rate while helping to remediate the underlying causes of slow reading.

Mechanical Devices

Finally, many mechanical devices can be used to increase reading rate and are often motivational for children, although no research exists to suggest that using them will provide greater gains than through nonmechanical approaches. These products all project text onto a screen or card and determine the time the child has to view the text or words. Many devices come with accompanying comprehension exercises. With most such devices, the reading time is gradually lessened until the child ceases to be able to complete the comprehension exercises at a predetermined level. Limited use of these products, as enjoyable novelties, can help to motivate children to increase the rate at which they process text. The Controlled Reader (Educational Developmental Laboratories), Tachomatic X500 (Psychotechnics), Reading Accelerator (Science Research Associates), Harvard University Reading Films (Harvard University Press), and Flash-X (Educational Developmental Laboratories) are examples.

SUMMARY

Technology, integrated into a literacy program with plenty of high-quality literature to foster reading and writing enjoyment, can be a powerful resource for teachers. Electronic books can provide yet another resource that provides reading practice and an authentic reason for repeated readings. Software programs that offer modeling of fluent reading and support for children struggling with decoding provide a confidence boost and a personal assistant. Comprehensive programs offering individualized reading lessons can encourage and monitor success using motivational graphs and incentives. Also, tachistoscopic devices are alternative resources that can flash words and phrases on a screen at increasingly rapid intervals. If such devices are used sparingly, they can invite children to increase their reading rate.

Although nothing can replace excellent direct instruction from an effective teacher, technological tools can be valuable resources in the elementary classroom, if integrated effectively into the existing literacy curriculum. Programs on the market today can offer small-group and individual reinforcement to repeated reading, fluency modeling, collaborative writing, and wide reading of literature—all activities found to increase reading and writing fluency. Perhaps the best reason to use technology to increase fluency, though, is the high level of engagement and motivation that children bring to technology-based tasks. For many children raised in the age of computers, positive literacy experiences on the computer can provide an easier transition to reading texts in traditional ways.

REFERENCES

AceReader (2005). AceReader [Computer Software]. Retrieved August 1, 2005 from www.acereader.com/ August 1, 2005.

Arthur's Teacher Troubles. (1993). Cambridge, MA: Random House/Broderbund.

Cochran-Smith, M. (1991). Word processing and writing in elementary class-rooms: A critical review of related literature. *Review of Educational Research, 61,* 107–155.

Davidson, M. R. (2003). *Read Naturally, scientific research, and reading first.* Portsmouth, NH: RMC Research Corporation.

Great Leaps Reading Program. Available from www.greatleaps.com.

Guthrie, J. T., & McCann, A. D. (1997). Characteristics of classrooms that pro-mote motivation and strategies for learning. In J. T. Guthrie & A. Wigfield (Eds.), *Reading engagement: Motivating readers through integrated instruc-tion* (pp. 128–148). Newark, DE: International Reading Association.

Illuminatus 4.5. (1999). Banbury, Oxon, United Kingdom: Digital Workshop.

KidPix. Available from http://rivapprod2.riverdeep.net/portal/page?_pageid= 336, 1&_dad=portal&_schema=PORTAL.

Labbo, L. D., Eakle, A. J., & Montero, M. K. (2002, May). Digital language experience approach: Using digital photographs and software as a language experience approach innovation. *ReadingOnline, 5*(8). Available at: www.readingonline.org/electronic/elecindex.asp?HREF=labbo2/Back.

Labbo, L. D., Leu, D. J., Kinzer, C. J., Teale, W. H., Cammack, D., Kara-Soteriou, J., & Sanny, R. (2003). Teacher wisdom stories: Cautions and recommendations for using computer-related technologies for literacy instruction. *The Reading Teacher, 57,* 300–304.

Labbo, L. D., & Reinking, D. (1999). Negotiating the multiple realities of tech-nology in literacy research and instruction. *Reading Research Quarterly, 34,* 478–493.

Landauer, T. (1995). *The trouble with computers.* Cambridge, MA: MIT Press.

The Learning Company. (1996). *Reader Rabbit series. Reading development Library 1.* Cambridge, MA: Author.

Lefever-Davis, S., & Pearman, C. (2005). Early readers and electronic texts: CD-ROM storybook features that influence reading behaviors. *The Reading Teacher, 58*(5), 446–454.

Leu, D. J. (1997). Caity's question: Literacy as deixis on the Internet. *The Reading Teacher, 23,* 62–67.

McKenna, M. C. (1998). Electronic texts and the transformation of beginning reading. In D. Reinking, M. McKenna, L. D. Labbo, & R. Kieffer (Eds.), *Handbook of literacy and technology: Transformations in a post-typo-graphic world* (pp. 45–59). Mahwah, NJ: Lawrence Erlbaum.

Meyer, M. (1996). *Just me and my dad.* New York: Big Tuna Media.

Oakley, G. (2002). Using CD-ROM "electronic talking books" to help children with mild reading difficulties improve their reading fluency. *Australian Journal of Reading Disabilities,* 7(4), 20–27.

Reading Speed Drills. Available from www.oxtonhouse.com/Fluency/SpDrills/spdrills.html.

Samuels, S. J. (2002). Reading fluency: Its development and assessment. In A. Farstrup & S. J. Samuels (Eds.), *What research has to say about reading instruction* (3rd ed., pp. 166–183). Newark, DE: International Reading Association.

Soliloquy Reading Assistant. Available from www.soliloquylearning.com.

Start-to-Finish. Available from www.donjohnston.com.

Tompkins, G. (2005). *Literacy for the 21st century,* 4th ed. Upper Saddle River, NJ: Prentice Hall.

Wren, S. (2005). Computer software for reading instruction. *Developing research-based resources for the balanced reading teacher.* Available at: www.balancedreading.com/computer.html.

Fluency and Assessment 9

Without question, fluency is an essential component of successful reading, and the failure of children to become fluent readers can have repercussions throughout their lives. The need for assessment, leading to intervention that helps children achieve fluency, is clear and irrefutable (Regional Educational Laboratory, 2003).

Classroom teachers must continue to monitor the fluency competence of their students to make sure they are making strides in this important area.

FORMATIVE ASSESSMENT

Assessment in fluency is, ideally, an ongoing interface between assessment and resultant instruction; in other words, assessment should provide a teacher with a kind of "road map" for future instruction. "Formative" assessment is the most direct, ongoing link between assessment and instruction, as it proceeds immediately from teaching or modeling to direct observation of the children practicing the skill that has been modeled, and it then offers students the teacher's feedback. In the case of reading fluency, formative assessment revolves around continual observation. Throughout the process, teachers take anecdotal notes as the children read the passages that have previously been modeled for them. These notes are then often incorporated into a checklist that can be used to summarize the performance of each child in the area of fluency (see Exhibit 9.1).

Teachers model fluent reading for their students, and then the children are coached on the kind of fluent, expressive reading expected from them

exhibit 9.1 **Example of a teacher-developed checklist for fluency.**

Name			Date
	YES	**NO**	**COMMENTS**
Reads at a rate appropriate to the text	○	✓	Doesn't vary rate according to purpose for reading
Observes proper punctuation	○	✓	All except exclamation points
Reads with expression	✓	○	Always!
Groups words appropriately	○	✓	Uses three- or four-word chunks
Decodes words with automaticity	○	✓	Stumbles on multisyllable words
Has command of basic sight words	○	✓	Still confuses "wh" and "th" words

when they, in turn, read aloud. As teachers then listen to their students read, they offer a wide variety of formative feedback; this is differentiated for the needs of the individual child, as in the following instances:

- If a child's reading doesn't sound like normal speech, the teacher will demonstrate how to make the reading sound more conversational.
- If the phrasing is grouped inappropriately, the teacher models appropriate grouping and has the child echo the phrases.
- If a child does not vary his rate, the teacher shows him how an interpretive reading might be more meaningful if some phrases were read rapidly and others more slowly and thoughtfully.
- As children read, the teacher may provide coaching on raising the pitch of the voice for a bit of intense dialogue and lowering it for a passage in which the character is musing.
- While observing a child's reading, the teacher may point out how more careful attention to punctuation and word emphasis will make the meaning clearer, for example, for a child who reads, "Who ate all my potato chips? I am talking to you, Brandon!" in a monotone.

SUMMATIVE ASSESSMENT

In order to see how much progress has been made in reading fluency, teachers need to do more formalized, concise assessments that essentially recap what achievement has been made toward the fluency goals in the three areas of fluency: rate of reading, reading accuracy, and prosody. These more global assessments are called "summative assessments." The teacher must also determine that children are developing fluency in their ability to write. As teachers listen to their students read and observe students as they are writing, the best way to evaluate their fluency is to offer them formative assessment and also to summarize their assessments more formally.

The remainder of this chapter will address how to use summative assessments to measure growth in all areas of reading and writing, as well as offer ideas to involve children in their own progress by helping them to do their own self-evaluations of their reading fluency. This chapter also includes a summary of three formalized commercial assessment tools that are widely used to evaluate fluency as well as two means of assessing writing fluency.

Assessing Reading Rate

Teachers need to assess children to determine the answer to this question: Do my students read haltingly or do they read quickly enough that they do not lose the meaning of what they are reading? The measurement of reading rate offers the most quantifiable method for assessing fluency, and it should take into account both the automaticity of word reading and reading speed in connected text (Hudson, Lane, & Pullen, 2005).

A slow, plodding reading rate may be symptomatic of a larger problem, however. In some cases, such awkward reading may be a sign that students view reading as "word calling" rather than truly understanding a written message. Or, if a child reads at grade level but her reading rate is low, lack of concern for reading faster may be the cause. Also, some slow readers may mistakenly believe that they must say every word completely and correctly in their heads in order to be proficient readers. A caveat is necessary here: Too much attention to reading rate may convince such readers that "good reading is fast reading" (Rasinski, 2003, p. 19), yet sometimes slow readers simply need some specific instruction to encourage them to move along more quickly and automatically.

Before reading rate is assessed and exercises are introduced to address an intervention, it is helpful for teachers to know what rates are appropriate for specific grade levels. These words-per-minute rates and published oral-reading-fluency norms are provided in Exhibit 9.2. The rates, with percentiles of students who normally reach those scores, are categorized into WCPM (words correct per minute) norms for the fall, winter, and spring of the academic year. Teachers can use these norms as benchmarks as they establish beginning-of-the-school-year baseline information about the fluency of their students.

Underlying Problems Causing Slow Reading Rate

Although reading rate will often improve automatically with the practice that much recreational reading provides, some specific problems may need to be addressed before the rate of reading can be improved, no matter what level at which the child is reading. These concerns include

- word-by-word reading
- finger pointing
- subvocalization
- difficulty making the return sweep from one line to the next
- slowness in decoding unfamiliar words
- too many regressive eye movements
- undiagnosed visual problems
- lack of a perceived need to read any faster (a pervasive reason for reading slowly)

exhibit 9.2 Oral reading fluency norms.

Grade	Percentile	Fall WCPM	Winter WCPM	Spring WCPM
2	75	82	106	124
	50	53	78	94
	25	23	46	65
3	75	107	123	142
	50	79	93	114
	25	65	70	87
4	75	125	133	143
	50	99	112	118
	25	72	89	92
5	75	126	143	151
	50	105	118	128
	25	77	93	100

(50th percentile for the upper grades: 125–150 wcpm)

Source: From Curriculum-based oral-fluency norms for students in grades 2–5 by J. E. Hasbrouck and G. Tindal, *Teaching Exceptional Children,* volume 24, 2005, pages 41–44. Copyright 1992 by The Council for Exceptional Children. Reprinted with permission.

Except for the visual concerns, which should be referred to a vision specialist, each of the other issues can be addressed using the following three approaches (other approaches have been mentioned in other chapters):

1. Offer children large amounts of material at their independent reading level and encourage them to reread the material repeatedly, for different purposes. As they are able to anticipate what is coming next in the material, they begin to move their eyes along more smoothly, thus reading more rapidly.

2. Actively encourage children to read faster by using their index finger as a guide to more effective eye movements. Using independent-level reading material, children can read a page of material as rapidly as they feel comfortable while moving their index finger down the center of the page (rather than under each individual word, which promotes word-by-word reading). In this manner, they force their

eyes to take in more words and phrases, rather than languishing on individual words.

3. Print words and phrases on index cards and flash them quickly for children, at faster and faster rates, and ask children to recollect what they saw. This approach causes children to decode more rapidly and in the phrase clusters that reflect natural oral-speech patterns. Commercial mechanical devices are also available for the purpose of flashing words and phrases to children. Computer programs, the Flash-X and the Controlled Reader (both by Educational Developmental Laboratories), Tachomatic X500 (Psychotechnics), and the Reading Accelerator (Science Research Associates) are all devices sold commercially that are designed to encourage children to read words and phrases more rapidly (see also Chapter 8).

Timed Readings

If problems listed above have been remediated, children can increase their reading rate and fluency via *timed readings*. The most widely used method to assess, and also increase, a child's reading rate is to have a child read a specified passage and see how much can be read in one minute (Samuels, 1979). Timed readings differ from traditional silent reading time in that, using this method, the teacher selects a reading passage and the children read the passage and then answer comprehension questions about what they have read (Fox, 2003). The purpose of such an instructional strategy is that children work on increasing their fluency and reading rate, but never at the expense of comprehension.

To initiate a timed reading, each child should be given a short passage (100–300 words, depending on the grade level) just below her instructional reading level. For each passage, the teacher should design a set of 10 multiple-choice comprehension questions (graded passages from a commercial informal reading inventory can be used for this purpose). The teacher can simply ask the child to read out loud and, at the end of 60 seconds, tell the child to stop. The teacher then counts the number of words that were read. This is the reader's rate in words per minute (WPM). More accurate fluency scores may be obtained when the teacher uses the average of two or three fluency readings from two or three different passages (Bos & Vaughn, 2002). As children's reading rate increases, comprehension is assessed to be sure that it has not been compromised by the increased speed. The results can be graphed to show a child's reading-fluency growth over time.

Children can also do their own reading-rate assessments and chart their progress over time. For this variation, the teacher should use a clock, a watch with a second hand, or a stopwatch to time children as they read a passage silently, and then keep track of the minutes that have gone by on the chalk board. As children finish, they raise their hands and the teacher tells them exactly how many seconds it took them to complete the passage. Children write that amount of time at the top of their papers. The teacher helps children to find their personal reading rate using the following formula:

Number of words in passage x 60 divided by number of seconds =
Rate in words per minute

When children have figured out their reading rate, or the words they have read per minute, they answer 10 comprehension questions; the teacher then corrects these questions and puts the number correctly answered at the top of the child's paper. Each child should have two charts to allow him to keep track of his growth in reading rate as well as comprehension, such as the ones shown in Exhibit 9.3.

Exhibit 9.3 shows charts that a third-grade girl used to show her progress in reading rate and comprehension. One can see that after reading three timed passages, the child's rate began to improve significantly, going from 39 wpm to 63 wpm. After reading seven passages, her comprehension also showed a marked improvement—going from 50 percent

exhibit 9.3 N'Issa's progress in reading.

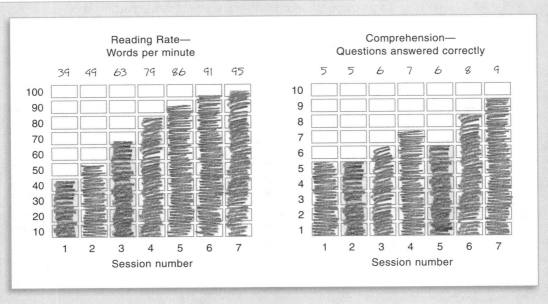

to 90 percent, as the child was able to concentrate more on the content of what she was reading and less on increasing her reading rate.

Assessing Accuracy

Teachers need to assess their students to be able to answer the questions:

- Is each of my students able to decode words accurately?
- Do they have a large store of words that they can recognize automatically, by sight?

Measurement of children's word-reading accuracy can take many forms. The Nonword Reading Test (Exhibit 9.4) and the Regularity Test (Exhibit 9.5) can quickly assess children's reading of words in isolation. For determining how a child reads words in context, simply listening to each child's oral reading and counting the number of errors per 100 words can provide valuable information about the child's reading accuracy, which is helpful for the future selection of texts for individual instructional purposes or for small-group instruction. A more thorough assessment providing more detailed information about why a particular child lacks reading accuracy can be obtained through a running record.

Running Records

Running records (Clay, 2000) can be used with any material a child is reading, making it an adaptable method for assessing oral-reading behaviors. As long as the teacher has paper and a pencil handy while observing the child reading, a running record of that reading can be made and later scored and analyzed. A tape recording allows the performance to be reviewed to verify the codings and scoring estimated during the assessment. The child continues reading until she reaches the criteria associated with the frustration level. At this point, in addition to not achieving a minimum of accuracy in word recognition and comprehension, the child usually exhibits other behavioral symptoms, such as sighing or squirming in her chair. The teacher then listens to the tape, calculates the percentage of words the child read correctly, and analyzes the miscues or errors. The teacher may make a series of check marks on a sheet of paper as the child reads each word correctly, and use other marks to indicate words the child either substitutes, repeats, pronounces incorrectly, or needs to have pronounced by the examiner. While teachers can make the running record on a blank sheet of paper, it is far easier to photocopy the page(s) of text the child will read and mark the running record next to or on top of the actual text that the child has read (see Exhibit 9.6 for an example of a running record).

exhibit 9.4 The Nonword Reading Test.

Directions: Print these words individually on cards and present them in random order for the child to read aloud. Record all reading responses.

Either a regular or an irregular pronunciation is acceptable, i.e., if "jint" is read rhyming with "lint" it is regular whereas if "jint" is read as rhyming with "pint" it is irregular; "soser" read as "soaser" is regular, rhyming with "loser" is irregular.

TEST ITEMS	
One Syllable	*Two Syllables*
plood	louble
aund	hausage
wolt	soser
jint	pettuce
hign	kolice
pove	skeady
wamp	dever
cread	biter
slove	islank
fongue	polonel
nowl	narine
swad	kiscuit
chove	
duede	
sworf	
jase	
freath	
warg	
choiy	

For 7 year olds, a score below 3 falls significantly below the norm.

For 10 year olds, a score below 26 on one-syllable words and 7 on two-syllable words falls significantly below the norm.

Source: Snowling, M. J., Stackhouse, J., and Rack, J. P. (1986). Phonological dyslexia and dysgraphia: A developmental analysis. *Cognitive Neuropsychology, 3,* 309–339, by kind permission of Psychology Press, www.psypress.co.uk/journals.asp, 2006

exhibit 9.5 The Regularity Test.

Directions: Print these words individually on cards and present them in random order for the child to read aloud. Record all reading responses.

TEST ITEMS			
Regular		*Irregular*	
One Syllable	*Two Syllables*	*One Syllable*	*Two Syllables*
seige	bitter	choir	double
grill	thimble	flood	sausage
drug	tutor	aunt	loser
slot	lobster	wolf	lettuce
lime	market	pint	police
film	divine	sign	steady
task	organ	dove	lever
shin	lemon	wand	liter
hatch	trumpet	bread	island
spade	mixture	glove	colonel
prince	rubber	tongue	marine
plug	tumble	bowl	biscuit
blade		swan	
bleat		shove	
snail		suede	
globe		sword	
cask		vase	
match		breath	
sand		ward	

For 7 year olds, a score below 7 on regular words and 3 on irregular words falls below the norm.

For 10 year olds, a score below 26 on regular words and 21 on irregular words falls below the norm.

Source: Snowling, M. J., Stackhouse, J., and Rack, J. P. (1986). Phonological dyslexia and dysgraphia: A developmental analysis. *Cognitive Neuropsychology, 3,* 309–339, by kind permission of Psychology Press, www.psypress.co.uk/journals.asp, 2006

exhibit 9.6 **Example of a running record.**

The first thing you must do when you ✓ ✓ ✓ ✓ ✓ ✓ $\frac{what}{when}$ ✓

wash your dog is to find him. Some ✓ ✓ ✓ ✓ ✓ ✓ ✓ ✓

dogs do not like to take baths. Use a ✓ ✓ ✓ ✓ ✓ ✓ $\frac{bats}{baths}$ ✓ ✓

hose. Get the dog very wet. Then put $\frac{horse}{hose}$ ✓ ✓ ✓ ✓ ✓ ✓ ✓

some doggy shampoo on him. Rinse ✓ ✓ $\frac{shan-}{shampoo}$ ✓ $\frac{Ring}{Rinse}$ ✓

him really well. Then dry him off. That ✓ ✓ $\frac{will}{well}$ ✓ ✓ ✓ ✓ ✓

is the part your dog will like the best! ✓ ✓ ✓ ✓ ✓ ✓ ✓ ✓ ✓

Give him a reward for letting you give ✓ ✓ ✓ $\frac{roar}{reward}$ ✓ $\frac{let}{letting}$ ✓ ✓

him the bath. ✓ ✓ ✓

ANALYSIS

Total words:	67	*Chelsea H.*
Deviations from text:	8	*Name of student*
Accuracy level:	84%	
	(frustration level)	*WPM (words per minute)*

This child read the text in a halting, word-by-word manner. After reading, the child was able to give the main idea of the text but was unable to recall details due to the errors in decoding of key words. Her errors were:

Substitutions: what/when   roar/reward   ring/rinse   let/letting

                    horse/hose   will/well   bats/baths

Mispronunciations: shan-/shampoo

Most of her errors affected comprehension because they made no sense, semantically or syntactically, in the sentences. A series of mini-lessons on using the context to help decode unfamiliar words is recommended.

Source: Cecil (2003).

After identifying the words that the child read incorrectly, the teacher calculates the percentage of words read correctly. The teacher uses the percentage of words correctly read to determine whether the book or reading material is too easy, too difficult, or appropriate for the child to read at this time. If the child reads 95 percent of the words accurately, the text is easy or at the independent reading level for that child. If the child reads between 90 and 94 percent of the words accurately, the text is at the child's instructional level. If the child reads fewer than 90 percent of the words accurately, the material is at the child's frustration level. The teacher should terminate the running-record assessment by asking the child to retell the story or the information in the passage that was read to determine if comprehension took place, and to underscore that understanding the text is always the main focus of reading.

Teachers should also use the information gained from the running record to determine what word-recognition strengths and needs the child possesses; mini-lessons can then be designed to develop the needs, which will result in more accurate reading. Finally, the teacher can categorize the child's miscues or errors according to how they affected the meaning of the passage. As teachers do this for each miscue or error, they can ask themselves the following questions (Tompkins, 2004):

- Did the child correct the error or miscue?
- Does the miscue change the meaning of the sentence?
- Does the miscue look or sound like the word in the text?
- Is the miscue grammatically similar to the word in the text?

Assessing Prosody

Finally, teachers must assess children in order to answer the following question: Is each of my students able to chunk words into phrases, heed punctuation, and read with appropriate expression that approximates conversational speech? The best way for teachers to assess a child's prosody is to listen to the child read aloud and use a checklist to determine if the reading contains the qualities that comprise fluent, expressive reading. The NAEP used four levels to distinguish fluent from disfluent reading (see Exhibit 9.7). Teachers can use these four levels to determine the reading prosody level of each of the learners in their class. By the end of second grade, children should have reached Level 4. Although most children can benefit from prosody instruction, such instruction would be deemed critical for those children scoring below Level 4 after second grade (U. S. Department of Education, 1995). Teachers need to be cautioned not to overinterpret the reading-rate norms, however, especially with children for whom English is a second language.

exhibit 9.7 Oral reading prosody scale.

LEVEL 4   Most reading is speechlike and consists of logical phrase groups that vary in length as appropriate. A few repetitions, regressions, and deviations from text may occur but do not change the meaning of the text. Syntax is intact. Most of the text is read with appropriate expression and intonation.

LEVEL 3   Most reading is in phrase groups of three or four words and sometimes fewer, but most phrasing appears appropriate and usually keeps the author's meaning and syntax intact. Little expression or appropriate intonation is noted.

LEVEL 2   Most reading is in two-word phrases, with some three- or four-word groupings. Occasional word-by-word reading is evident. Word groupings are at times awkward and appear not to follow the larger context of the sentence or the passage.

LEVEL 1   Most reading is word-by-word. Occasionally, several-word phrases are used, but these are rare and do not consider the author's meaning or syntax.

Source: Adapted from U.S. Department of Education (1995).

Self-Evaluation of Reading Fluency

For an assessment program in fluency to produce results, it must be indelibly tied to future instruction. In order for that to occur, the focus of the assessment—the children—should be integrally involved in the assessment process. Besides the informal formative assessment procedures that entail coaching from the teacher, mentioned earlier in the chapter, children can be taught to ask their own questions about their reading. To use these questions, first discuss each of them with children. Then allow children to read a passage into a tape recorder and play it back, listening reflectively to their reading and answering each of the questions. Children can also use these questions to initiate this process with partners so that both begin to internalize the qualities that create smooth, meaningful oral reading (see Exhibit 9.8 for fluency questions that can be used for self-evaluation).

exhibit 9.8 Fluency questions for self-evaluation.

Name: _____   Date: _____

○ Did my reading sound like real speech, like people talk? Would someone listening understand what the author meant from my reading?

○ Did I have to work hard to pronounce the words correctly? Did I make many mistakes in my reading? When I made a mistake that changed the meaning, did I go back and change it?

○ Did I read with good expression or in a monotone? Did I vary my volume when appropriate to express meaning? Was I reading loudly enough?

○ Did I change speed when necessary, especially when I wanted to stress certain parts? Did I read too slowly? Did I read too quickly?

○ Did I group the words correctly? Did I pay attention to periods to make my voice go down? Did I pause for commas? Did my voice go up for question marks? Did I sound excited for exclamation marks? Did I emphasize any words that needed it?

○ What is best about my reading? What should I work on to make my reading even better?

Source: Adapted from Rasinski (2003).

Formal Standardized Assessments

Widely used standardized assessments on the market today provide summative data about children's reading fluency. These commercial instruments provide information about their validity (do they measure what they intend to measure?) and their reliability (are the results consistent over multiple administrations?) These assessment devices can be especially helpful in providing valuable information about the fluency needs of the class, but decisions about instructional needs of individuals should always be made in conjunction with daily, ongoing assessment of each child's reading.

Dynamic Indicators of Basic Early Literacy (DIBELS)

One such assessment is Dynamic Indicators of Basic Early Literacy (DIBELS; available from Sopris West, www.sopriswest.com). DIBELS includes a subtest of Oral Reading Fluency and Retell Fluency for children in the first through third grades. The Oral Reading Fluency is standardized and individually administered. Children read a passage aloud for one minute, and then the number of correct words per minute is determined to attain the oral-reading-fluency rate. The Retell Fluency is a measure of comprehension that goes with the Oral Reading Fluency assessment.

The Gray Oral Reading Test, Fourth Edition (GORT-4)

A second formalized assessment device, the Gray Oral Reading Test, Fourth Edition (GORT-4; from PRO-ED, www.proedinc.com), is a norm-referenced measure of oral-reading performance. Skills assessed include rate, accuracy, fluency (rate and accuracy combined), comprehension, and overall reading ability (rate, accuracy, and comprehension combined).

Test of Word Reading Efficiency (TOWRE)

A third formalized assessment is the Test of Word Reading Efficiency (TOWRE; also from PRO-ED), a nationally normed measure of word reading accuracy and fluency. Because it can be administered quickly, the test provides an efficient means of monitoring the growth of two kinds of word reading skills that are critical in the development of overall reading ability: the ability to accurately recognize familiar words as whole units or "sight words," and the ability to "sound out" words rapidly. No accompanying test of comprehension is included.

Assessing Writing Fluency

As previously discussed, one facet of writing fluency is the ability to write accurately and rapidly. Evaluating the complexity of a child's writing can provide insight into the level of difficult words that child feels comfortable using when composing, but, until recently, no objective assessment of children's word-writing skills could be given to a whole class at one time. Moreover, no assessment device was available that considered children's accuracy, complexity, and fluency in their ability to generate words. A new tool, the Word Writing CAFÉ (Leal, 2005; CAFÉ stands for Complexity, Accuracy, Fluency Evaluation), was developed to allow teachers to objectively evaluate their students' word-writing ability in terms of fluency, accuracy, and complexity in grades 1–6. Through scoring and tracking their students' progress through the school year, teachers can use the assessment data to understand and improve students' word writing.

To administer the Word Writing CAFÉ, each child in the class is given a piece of paper on which three columns of ten boxes are drawn. Children are then asked to write down as many words as they can think of in ten minutes (see Exhibit 9.9 for an example of a completed form). The words are then scored according to the following steps:

exhibit 9.9 Completed CAFÉ form.

1st/2nd

Name		Date		Teacher	
The	I	dad	I	sun	I
see	I	mom	I	~~mun~~	
They	I	two	I	your	I
Then	I	too	I	~~#~~ I six	
~~Thes~~		to	I	ran	I
you	I	grandma	2	~~playd~~	
yes	I	grandpa	2	play	I
no	I	~~#~~ cat ~~hat~~	I	~~sally~~ ~~bally~~	
on	I	day ~~hog~~	I		
can	I	Boo!	I		

TW: 28   CW: 24   1S: 22   2S: 2
3S: ____   4S: ____   5S: ____   6S: ____

Source: Leal, Dorothy J. (2005, Dec./2006, Jan.). The Word Writing CAFÉ: Assessing student writing for complexity, accuracy, and fluency. *The Reading Teacher, 59* (4), 340–350. Reprinted with permission of Dorothy J. Leal and the International Reading Association. All rights reserved.

- To determine *fluency:* Count the total number of boxes with any writing in them. Anything counts as a word, except scribbles or pictures. This is the TW (total words) figure.
- To determine *accuracy:* Cross out misspelled words, duplicated words, proper names, and numbers that are not spelled out. This is the CW (correct words) figure.
- To determine *complexity:* Count the number of syllables in each correctly spelled word. Using the blanks provided, fill in the number of one syllable words (1s), and so on.

When national benchmarks are complete, the Word Writing CAFÉ will enable teachers to see how their students compare nationally in terms of word fluency, accuracy, and complexity. At the time of this writing, however, the assessment device is in its pilot form.

The creator of the Word Writing CAFÉ offers the following important caveats to consider when administering this helpful tool:

- Use the tool to track student progress, not to assign student grade-level abilities.

- Be sure the assessment is administered in a nonprint environment to make sure that children do not copy from word walls or other print displays.

- Use only the following prompts to give children ideas of what to write:

  "Write words that tell what you like to do and where you like to go."

  "Write words that describe what you can see, hear, smell, taste, or feel."

  "Write words that tell what is in your house or school."

  "Write any word that you know how to read or write."

Although the Word Writing CAFÉ offers a way for teachers to see strengths and needs in children's word writing and to evaluate how their teaching is affecting children's growth in fluency accuracy and word complexity, word writing is not the ultimate goal of any writing program; *authentic* writing for *authentic* purposes is. Much as teachers assess children's reading by listening to them read, teachers can also assess writing fluency by observing their students as they write. Formative assessment, which focuses on the processes that writers use, occurs as the teacher provides feedback while children are writing so they can use it to improve their writing. To accomplish this, anecdotal notes should be taken when children are in writer's workshop to determine which children settle down to the task easily and start writing, and which children struggle to think of ideas or are slowed down by problems with the conventions of writing. Teachers should note which children have problems with spelling and spend an inordinate amount of time sounding out words or asking for spelling assistance. Noted, too, should be how fluently each child is able to come up with creative ideas to write about, which children actually complete assigned writing tasks, and who seems willing to share written products.

A checklist, such as the example in Exhibit 9.10, can be created to facilitate recording observations of each child's writing fluency, and to incorporate the observations into a more summative assessment.

exhibit 9.10 Checklist for early writing fluency.

Date	LaQuinya	DeWayne	Hoa	Melik	Raul	Trent
Spelling						
Knows most grade-level words	○	○	○	○	○	○
Spells most words automatically	○	○	○	○	○	○
Doesn't labor over unknown words	○	○	○	○	○	○
Edits for Conventions						
Proofreads	○	○	○	○	○	○
Detects missing words/incomplete sentences	○	○	○	○	○	○
Circles misspelled words	○	○	○	○	○	○
Punctuation is appropriate	○	○	○	○	○	○
Grammar is correct	○	○	○	○	○	○
Margins/paragraphs are correct	○	○	○	○	○	○
Handwriting is legible	○	○	○	○	○	○
Speed						
Writes quickly	○	○	○	○	○	○
Completes writing tasks	○	○	○	○	○	○
Seems to write with ease	○	○	○	○	○	○
Ideas						
Quickly finds ideas for writing tasks	○	○	○	○	○	○
Usually has a writing "agenda"	○	○	○	○	○	○
Responds to teacher-directed topics	○	○	○	○	○	○
Begins a new writing project soon after completing one	○	○	○	○	○	○
Pieces are begun/finished/published	○	○	○	○	○	○
Uses a variety of genres	○	○	○	○	○	○
Personal narrative	○	○	○	○	○	○
Fiction	○	○	○	○	○	○
Poetry	○	○	○	○	○	○
Informational	○	○	○	○	○	○
Attitude						
Sees him/herself as a writer	○	○	○	○	○	○
Enjoys writing	○	○	○	○	○	○
Shows pride in finished products	○	○	○	○	○	○
Volunteers to share written products	○	○	○	○	○	○

SUMMARY

In any quality reading program there should be a synergy between assessment and instruction; in other words, assessment should inform the teacher about what should be taught or reinforced, while teaching should give the teacher insights into specific areas about where more information is needed. This chapter has outlined both formative and summative approaches to assessing the major components of fluency—rate, accuracy, and prosody, as well as writing fluency—in a manner that leads the teacher to determine more clearly the next step needed in classroom instruction.

REFERENCES

Allington, R. L. (1984). Fluency: The neglected goal in reading instruction. *The Reading Teacher, 36,* 556–561.

Bos, C. S., & Vaughn, S. (2002). *Strategies for teaching children with learning and behavior problems,* 5th ed. Boston: Allyn & Bacon.

Cecil, N. L. (2003). *Striking a balance: Best practices for early literacy.* Scottsdale, AZ: Holcomb Hathaway.

Clay, M. (2000). *Running records for classroom teachers.* Portsmouth, NH: Heinemann.

Fox, B. J. (2003). *Word recognition activities: Patterns and strategies for developing fluency.* Upper Saddle River, NJ: Merrill.

Fuchs, L. S., Fuchs, D., Hamlett, C. L., Waltz, L., & Germann, G. (1993). Formative evaluation of academic progress: How much growth can we expect? *School Psychology Review, 22,* 27–48.

Hasbrouck, J. E., & Tindal, G. (1992). Curriculum-based oral-fluency norms for students in grades 2–5. *Teaching Exceptional Children, 24,* 41–44.

Hudson, R. F., Lane, H. B., & Pullen, P. C. (2005). Reading fluency assessment and instruction: What, why, and how? *The Reading Teacher, 58,* 704–714.

Leal, D. J. (2005). The Word Writing CAFÉ: Assessing student writing for complexity, accuracy, and fluency. *The Reading Teacher, 59,* 340–350.

Rasinski, T. V. (2003). Beyond speed: Reading fluency is more than reading fast. *California Reader, 2,* 5–11.

Regional Educational Laboratory. (2003). *A focus on fluency.* Honolulu, HI: Pacific Resources for Education and Learning.

Samuels, S. J. (1979). The method of repeated readings. *The Reading Teacher, 32,* 403–408.

Snowling, M. J., Stackhouse, J., & Rack, J. P. (1986). Phonological dyslexia and dysgraphia: A developmental analysis. *Cognitive Neuropsychology, 3,* 309–339.

Tompkins, G. E. (2004). *Literacy for the 21st century: A balanced approach,* 3d ed. Upper Saddle River, NJ: Merrill Prentice Hall.

U.S. Department of Education. (1995). *Listening to children read aloud.* Washington, D.C.: National Center for Education Statistics.

Appendices

Appendix A

CHILDREN'S LITERATURE RESOURCES

Children's Literature for Oral Reading

Alexander, L. *The Remarkable Journey of Prince Jen.* New York: Dutton, 1991.

Baker, J. *Where the Forest Meets the Sea.* New York: Greenwillow, 1988.

Baker, J. *Window.* New York: Greenwillow, 1991.

Cosby, B. *Money Troubles.* New York: Scholastic, 1998.

Creech, S. *The Wanderer.* New York: HarperCollins, 2000.

Danziger, P. *Amber Brown Is Not a Crayon.* New York: Putnam, 1994.

Daugherty, J. *Poor Richard.* New York: Viking, 1941.

Emberley, B. *Drummer Hoff.* Illustrated by E. Emberley. New York: Prentice Hall, 1967.

Fleishman, P. *Bull Run.* New York: HarperCollins, 1993.

Freedman, R. *The Wright Brothers: How They Invented the Airplane.* New York: Holiday, 1991.

Fritz, J. *What's the Big Idea, Ben Franklin?* Illustrated by M. Tomes. New York: Coward, McCann, 1978.

Grifalconi, A. *Darkness and the Butterfly.* Boston: Little, Brown, 1987.

Ho, M. *Hush! A Thai Lullaby.* Illustrated by H. Meade. New York: Orchard, 1996.

Hoberman, M. A. *You Read to Me, I'll Read to You: Very Short Stories to Read Together.* Illustrated by M. Emberley. Boston: Little, Brown, 2001.

Hooks, W. H. *Moss Gown.* Illustrated by D. Carrick. New York: Houghton Mifflin, 1987.

Houston, G. *My Great-Aunt Arizona.* Illustrated by S. C. Lamb. New York: HarperCollins, 1992.

Jaques, B. *Pearls of Lutra: A Tale for Redwall.* New York: Philomel, 1997.

Kellogg, S. *A Penguin Pup for Pinkerton.* New York: Dial, 2001.

Lamb, C., and Mary Lamb. *Tales from Shakespeare,* rev. ed. New York: Children's Classics, 1986.

L'Engle, Madeline. *A Wrinkle in Time.* New York: Farrar, Straus & Giroux, 1962.

Levine, E. *The Tree That Would Not Die.* Illustrated by T. Rand. New York: Scholastic, 1995.

Lewis, C. S. *The Lion, the Witch, and the Wardrobe.* Illustrated by P. Baynes. New York: Macmillan, 1950.

Lobel, A. *Frog and Toad Are Friends.* New York: HarperCollins, 1970.

Lobel, A. *Frog and Toad Together.* New York: HarperCollins, 1979.

McCloskey, R. *Make Way for Ducklings.* New York: Viking, 1941.

McPhail, D. *The Dream Child.* New York: Dutton, 1985.

Meltzer, M. *Benjamin Franklin: The New American.* New York: Watts, 1988.

Micucci, C. *The Life and Times of the Apple.* New York: Orchard, 1992.

Micucci, C. *The Life and Times of the Peanut.* Boston: Houghton Mifflin, 1997.

Milne, A. A. *Winnie-the-Pooh.* Illustrated by E. H. Shepard. New York: Dutton, 1954.

Moss, L. *Zin! Zin! Zin! A Violin.* Illustrated by M. Priceman. New York: Simon & Schuster, 1995.

Nesbit, E. *Beautiful Stories from Shakespeare.* New York: Weathervane, 2004 (facsimile of 1907 edition).

Parish, P. *Amelia Bedelia.* New York: HarperCollins, 1992.

Potter, Beatrix. *The Tales of Peter Rabbit.* New York: Warne, 1902.

Rosen, M. *We're Going on a Bear Hunt.* Illustrated by H. Oxenbury. New York: Macmillan, 1989.

Sachar, L. *Marvin Redpost: Kidnapped at Birth?* New York: Random House, 1992.

Sachar, L. *Holes.* New York: Farrar, Straus & Giroux, 1998.

San Souci, R. D. *Young Merlin.* New York: Doubleday, 1990.

Sendak, Maurice. *Where the Wild Things Are.* New York: Harper & Row, 1963.

Seuss, Dr. *The 500 Hats of Bartholomew Cubbins.* New York: Vanguard, 1938.

Seuss, Dr. *The Cat in the Hat.* New York: Random House, 1957.

Sperry, A. *Call It Courage.* New York: Macmillan, 1940.

Twain, Mark. *Adventures of Huckleberry Finn.* Edited by W. Blair and V. Fischer. Berkeley: University of California Press, 1985.

Van Rynbach, I. *Everything from a Nail to a Coffin.* New York: Orchard Books, 1991.

Von Tscharner, R., and R. L. Fleming. *New Providence: A Changing Cityscape.* Illustrated by D. Orloff. San Diego: Harcourt Brace Jovanovich, 1987.

Whelan, G. *Homeless Bird*. New York: HarperCollins, 2000.

White, E. B. *Charlotte's Web*. Illustrated by G. Williams. New York: Harper & Row, 1952.

Willard, N. *Night Story*. Illustrated by I. Plume. San Diego: Harcourt Brace Jovanovich, 1981.

Yolen, J. *Owl Moon*. Illustrated by J. Schoenherr. New York: Philomel, 1987.

Books for Poetry and Choral Reading

Ada, A. F., Harris, V., & Hopkins, L. B. *A Chorus of Cultures Anthology*. Carmel, CA: Hampton Brown, 1993.

Fleishman, P. *I Am Phoenix*. New York: HarperCollins, 1985.

Fleishman, P. *Joyful Noise*. New York: HarperCollins, 1988.

Fleishman, P. *Big Talk: Poems for Four Voices*. Cambridge, MA: Candlewick Press, 2000.

Florian, D. *Bing Bang Bong*. San Diego: Harcourt Brace, 1994.

Greenfield, E. *Honey, I Love*. New York: Harper & Row, 1978.

Herrera, J. F. *Laughing Out Loud, I Fly: Poems in English and Spanish*. New York: HarperCollins, 1988.

Holbrook, S. *The Dog Ate My Homework*. Honesdale, PA: Boyds Mills Press, 1996.

Holbrook, S. *Which Way to the Dragon!: Poems for the Coming-On-Strong*. Honesdale, PA: Boyds Mills Press, 1997.

Hughes, L. *The Dreamkeeper and Other Poems*. New York: Knopf, 1932/1994.

Johnston, T. *My Mexico–Mexico Mio*. New York: Penguin Putnam, 1996.

Kushkin, K. *Near the Window Tree*. New York: Harper & Row, 1975.

Kushkin, K. *Dogs and Dragons, Trees and Dreams*. New York: HarperCollins, 1980.

Lewis, J. P. *The Little Buggers: Insect and Spider Poems*. New York: Dial, 1998.

Mora, P. *Confetti: Poems for Children*. New York: Lee & Low, 1999.

Morrison, L. *The Break Dance Kids: Poems of Sports, Motion, and Locomotion*. New York: Lothrop, Lee & Shepard, 1985.

Nye, N. S. *The Tree Is Older Than You Are*. New York: Simon & Schuster, 1995.

Pappas, T. *Math Talk: Mathematical Ideas in Poems for Two Voices*. San Carlos, CA: Wide World/Tetra, 1991.

Prelutsky, J. *The New Kid on the Block*. New York: Greenwillow, 1984.

Prelutsky, J. *Tyrannosaurus Was a Beast: Dinosaur Poems*. New York: Greenwillow, 1988.

Shields, C. D. *Lunch Money*. New York: Dutton, 1995.

Sierra, J. *Antarctic Antics: A Book of Penguin Poems*. San Diego: Gulliver, 1998.

Silverstein, S. *Where the Sidewalk Ends*. New York: HarperCollins, 1974.

Silverstein, S. *A Light in the Attic*. New York: HarperCollins, 1981.

Soto, G. *Neighborhood Odes*. San Diego: Harcourt Brace, 1992.

Soto, G. *Canto Familiar*. San Diego: Harcourt Brace, 1995.

Wong, J. *A Suitcase of Seaweed*. New York: Simon & Schuster, 1996.

Yolen, J. *Weather Report*. Honesdale, PA: Wordsong, 1993.

Yolen, J. *Water Music*. Honesdale, PA: Wordsong, 1995.

Songbooks

Andrews, G. *Creative Rhythmic Movement for Children*. Englewood Cliffs, NJ: Prentice-Hall, 1954.

Bertail, I. *The Complete Nursery Song Book*. New York: Lothrop, Lee & Shepard, 1954.

Classics for Children and Introduction to the Orchestra. ABC School Supply, Inc., P.O. Box 4750, Norcross, GA 30091. Cassette No. 266–125–71 (Nutcracker Suite and more).

Deluxe Rhythm Sets. ABC School Supply, Inc., P.O. Box 4750, Norcross, GA 30091. Record No. 549–259–71.

Grammer, R. *Teaching Peace Songbook and Teacher's Guide*. Brewerton, NY: Red Note Records, 2005.

Jenkins, E. *Adventures in Rhythm*. ABC School Supply, Inc., P.O. Box 4750, Norcross, GA 30091. Record No. 404–950–71.

Jenkins, E. *Counting Games and Game Songs for the Little Ones*. New York: Scholastic Records, 1965.

Lauritzen, P. *Preschool Song Kit*. Rio Vista, CA: Ways and Means Curriculum, 1982.

Seeger, R. C. *American Folksongs for Children*. New York: Doubleday, 1948.

A Song Is a Rainbow (Words and music for over 50 tunes, plus puppet and felt board ideas). Opportunities for Learning, Inc., 20417 Nordhoff St., Dept. NB, Chatsworth, CA 91311. Record No. GP-16460.

Plays and Readers Theatre

Braun, C., & W. Braun. *Readers Theatre: Scripted Rhymes and Rhythms*. Winnipeg, MB: Portage & Main Press, 2000.

Braun, C., & W. Braun. *Readers Theatre: More Scripted Rhymes and Rhythms*. Winnipeg, MB: Portage & Main Press, 2001.

Braun, C., & W. Braun. *Readers Theatre: Treasury of Stories*. Winnipeg, MB: Portage & Main Press, 2002.

Braun, C., & W. Braun. *Readers Theatre for Young Children*. Winnipeg, MB: Portage & Main Press, 2004.

Dixon, N., A. Davies, & C. Politano. *Learning with Readers Theatre*. Winnipeg, MB: Portage & Main Press, 2001.

Gillies, E. *Creative Dramatics for All Children*. Washington, D. C. Association for Childhood Education International, 1973.

Haven, K. *Great Moments in Science: Experiments and Readers Theatre*. Englewood, CO: Teacher Ideas Press, 1996.

Murphy, D. *Revolutionary War Read-Aloud Plays*. New York: Scholastic, 2000.

Pugliano, C. *Easy-to-Read Folk and Fairy Tale Plays*. New York: Scholastic, 1998.

Pugliano-Martin, C. *25 Just-Right Plays for Emergent Readers*. New York: Scholastic, 1997.

Pugliano-Martin, C. *25 Emergent Reader Plays around the Year*. New York: Scholastic, 1999.

Pugliano-Martin, C. *Tall Tales Read-Aloud Plays*. New York: Scholastic, 2000.

Raczuk, H., & M. Smith. *Invitation to Readers Theatre*. Winnipeg, MB: Portage & Main Press, 2001.

Raczuk, H., & M. Smith. *Invitation to Readers Theatre Book 2*. Winnipeg, MB: Portage & Main Press, 2003.

Scher, A., & C. Verrall. *100+ Ideas for Drama*. Portsmouth, NH: Heinemann, 1985.

Appendix B

READING INTEREST INVENTORY

Directions: Have children write their responses in the blanks. For preliterate children, read the questions orally and transcribe their responses.

Name _____ Age _____ Grade _____

School _____ Date _____ Interviewer _____

1. What is your favorite television show?
   _____

2. Who is your favorite TV character? Why?
   _____
   _____

3. If you could make up a TV show, what would it be about?
   _____
   _____

4. What is your favorite movie? Why?
   _____
   _____

5. What is your favorite animal? Why?
   _____
   _____

6. Where have you traveled?
   _____
   _____
   _____

7. Name your three favorite places and tell why.
   _____
   _____
   _____

8. If you could have tickets for any place in the world, where would you go? Why?

9. If you had a time machine and could go to any place in the past or future, where would you go? Why?

10. What is your favorite subject in school? Why?

11. In what subject are you the best?

12. What is the latest book you read?

13. Did you enjoy it? Why or why not?

14. What magazines do you enjoy?

15. If it were a rainy day, what would you do at home?

16. If it were a sunny day, what would you do at home?

17. What is your favorite hobby?

18. What is your favorite sport?

19. If I gave you $100 to buy books, what books would you buy?

Appendix C

ELECTRONIC RESOURCES TO INCREASE FLUENCY

The Academy of Reading

www.autoskill.com

The Academy of Reading uses a consistent methodology and a dynamic intervention engine to help students achieve rapid and permanent gains in the five core areas outlined by the National Reading Panel, including reading fluency and automaticity.

Great Leaps Reading Program

www.greatleaps.com

This program has three components: a phonics improvement component; sight phrases designed to improve sight-reading rate and accuracy; and reading fluency passages that use age-appropriate stories to increase reading fluency through repeated reading.

Kurzweil Computer-Based Reading System

www.kurzweiledu.com

This program is designed to improve reading rate and accuracy. For each lesson in the series of readings, a controlled text is used and progress is analyzed using tape recordings. To progress to the next level of the language reader series, the student must achieve 80 percent accuracy in fluency and comprehension and a reading rate of 50 words per minute. A chart allows the teacher to record success for each student.

Odyssey Reading

www.compasslearning.com

The innovative technology in this program delivers research-based assessment aligned to the pre-K–12 language arts curriculum and comprehensive reporting for improved school achievement. The program meets critical aspects of No Child Left Behind legislation, including assessment and accountability for reading fluency.

Plato Focus on Reading and Language Program

www.plato.com

Featured here are more than 1,200 pages of printed curriculum, as well as a verbally interactive software component for supported fluency practice.

The software component also includes a classroom manager that allows the teacher to customize the phoneme order to correspond to the classroom's comprehensive reading program.

The Reader Rabbit Series

www.learningcompany.com

These electronic books use digitalized pronunciations of certain words and sentences to aid in reading accuracy; or the teacher may opt to have the entire story read aloud, offering the child a model of fluent reading while the child tracks along. On most illustrations, hot spots, which the child clicks on, cause characters to speak, animals to make appropriate sounds, and objects to move.

Reading Speed Drills

www.oxtonhouse.com

Word-list drills in this program are designed to promote reading fluency. The program is composed of two sets. One set contains 143 pages of word drills, including one-syllable words and phonetically irregular words. The second set contains 150 pages of word drills that cover one-syllable words and 114 phonetically irregular words.

Read Naturally

www.readnaturally.com

This website claims to provide teachers with all the tools they need in order to address the fluency requirements of their students. The package includes books, tapes, CDs, and software programs. A reading fluency table can be downloaded for free. Read Naturally offers six phonics levels, which include 24 nonfiction stories, and corresponding tapes and CDs. All the materials are sequenced. Materials for fluency assessment for grade 1 through grade 8 are also available.

Soliloquy Reading Assistant

www.soliloquylearning.com

Scientifically based speech recognition software is at the core of this program, which works like a classroom aide—reading stories aloud to model fluency and listening as the child reads aloud. The program also provides intervention when the student struggles, and it offers assistance with pronunciations and word meanings. It also addresses the fluency standards in Reading First, the national initiative in No Child Left Behind.

Author and Title Index

Subject Index

Diversity, of class, 69
Drafting, 87
Drama, 39–49 (*see also*
    Plays; Readers theatre)
  casting the actors, 48
  choral reading and, 37
  creating original, 47–48
Drop everything and read
    (DEAR), 74
Dyad reading, 60 (*see also*
    Assisted reading)
Dynamic Indicators of Basic
    Early Literacy
    (DIBELS), 130–131

Early literacy:
  choral reading and, 35–36
  plays for, 41
  writing and, 99–101,
    133–134
Echo reading, 31–32, 53–54
Editing, 88, 89
  checklist, 134
Electronic books, 105–109
    (*see also* Software)
E-mail dialogue journals, 97
English as a second language,
    see English language
    learners
English language learners, 16,
    19, 20, 22, 26, 28, 30,
    31, 35, 36, 40, 46, 49,
    59, 60, 78, 79, 80, 95,
    128
Enjoyment, reading for, 3
Environmental print, activity,
    82
Evaluation (*see also*
    Assessment):
  of taped reading, 13
  of writing fluency,
    131–134
  self-, of reading fluency,
    129–130
Exclamation mark, 29

Expository:
  discourse, 94, 95
  reading, 70
  writing, 93–95
Expression, reading with, 5

Feedback:
  formative, 118–119
  offering, 63–64
  software programs offer-
    ing, 110–111
Finger pointing, 120
Flash cards, 122
Flash-X program, 122
Fluency:
  assessment of, 117–135
    (*see also* Assessment)
  assisted reading and,
    51–64 (*see also* Assisted
    reading)
  checklist for, 118
  choral reading and,
    25–38 (*see also* Choral
    reading)
  coaches, 61–64 (*see also*
    Assisted reading)
  communicating with par-
    ents, 78–79
  defining, 3–5
  drama and, 39–49 (*see
    also* Plays; Readers the-
    atre)
  electronic resources,
    144–145 (*see also*
    Software)
  history of instruction, 5–6
  importance of, 2–3
  improving, 7–8
  in writing, 8 (*see also*
    Writing)
  modeling, 20–22 (*see also*
    Modeling)
  NIM and, 52–53, 54
  norms for oral reading,
    120, 121

oral reading and, *see* Oral
    reading
  phrase markings and,
    55–55
  practice and, 68
  reading commercial plays,
    40–42
  reading poetry and, 16–19
  self-evaluation of,
    129–130
  silent reading and, *see*
    Independent silent read-
    ing
  technology and, 103–114
    (*see also* Software;
    Technology)
  writing, *see* Writing
Fluency development lesson,
    14
Fluency-Oriented Reading
    Instruction (FORI),
    56–58
Folk tales, 41, 43
FORI, 56–58
Formative assessment,
    118–119
Free-reading time, 70–71

Goldilocks method, 71
Gray Oral Reading Test, 4e
    (GORT-4), 131
Great Leaps Reading
    Program, 110, 144
Guided practice sessions,
    writing, 97

Harvard University Reading
    Films, 114
Home, fostering reading at,
    76–82
Hot spots, in electronic
    books, 106

Illuminatus 4.5, 106–107
Imitative reading, 31–32